D0209738

REMEMBERING
AND
FORGETTING

REMEMBERING AND FORGETTING

AN INQUIRY INTO THE NATURE OF MEMORY

EDMUND BLAIR BOLLES

WALKER AND COMPANY
New York

First published in the United States of America
in 1988 by the Walker Publishing Company, Inc.

Published simultaneously in Canada by Thomas Allen & Son
Canada, Limited, Markham, Ontario.

Library of Congress Cataloging-in-Publication Data

Bolles, Edmund Blair, 1942–
Remembering and forgetting.

Includes index.
1. Memory. I. Title.
BF371.B59   1988   153.1'2   87-14791
ISBN 0-8027-1004-2

Printed in the United States of America

10 9 8 7 6 5 4 3 2 1

> flunked
> the
> third
> grade

Even if we count "ABCs" as one word, this list holds more words than rote learning can quickly permit, yet English speakers can learn it easily because it makes sense. If we organize the list alphabetically,

> ABCs
> after
> didn't
> flunked
> grade
> I
> I
> learn
> my
> the
> third
> until

it becomes harder to remember. Language is the most elaborate and universal organization of symbols, and the organizing principles of languages are their grammars. Grammars are neither logical nor consistent, and they are ambiguous, depending on context to determine meaning. Since the organization of other memories have these same anti-mathematical characteristics, we can call the organizing principle of any interpretive memory, linguistic or not, its grammar.

In the years following Miller's original work, repeated experiments have tested and expanded on Miller's observation. This research has confirmed a basic tenet of the Bartlett tradition: Meaningful order aids in recall. We can recall something in greater detail and with greater accuracy if it was organized originally according to a familiar grammar.

During the later 1960s and early 1970s the importance of organization turned up in the study of recognition as well. The original techniques of Ebbinghaus, Bartlett, and Miller tested for recall. They asked subjects to produce details from memory. Recognition can be tested by showing a subject a word and asking whether he remembers having seen it earlier in the experiment. For a long time the primary difference between this recognition test and recall experiments seemed to be that subjects did better in recognition studies.

The pioneer who brought recognition research into line with the Bartlett tradition was George Mandler, an Austrian-born psychologist now living in Canada. Mandler began his upheaval in recognition studies in the late 1960s by trying to clear up a few loose threads. Research had shown that recognition becomes confused when confronted with paired or categorically associated words. For example, if I present a list that includes the word *salt* and then, as part of a recognition test, show a subject the word *pepper,* he may say that he recognizes the second word as having appeared on the list.

Similar errors occur in recall tests. A person trying to remember a list may say *salt* when the list includes *pepper.* But Mandler found that confused recognition declines as the context of the words grows more orderly. We do not mistakenly recognize the word *pepper* if, instead of learning meaningless lists of words, we read the words in the context of a sentence like, "He sprinkled salt on his french fries." Meaningful organization makes confused recognition unlikely. Mandler also showed that if a subject fails to recall an item from a meaningful list, he will probably be uncertain about that same item in a recognition test. Furthermore, subjects sometimes recall certain items that were not on a meaningful list. For instance, if a subject were to read a list of George Washington's virtues and then asked to recite the list, the subject might say the word *courageous* even though it had not appeared. Mandler found that if he showed people meaningful lists and then tested for recognition, they were just as likely to recognize an intrusion like *courageous* as a word that had been on the list. Mandler established—and much research has confirmed—that the effects of meaning on memory are equal, whether tested by recall or by recognition methods.

The work of Bartlett, Miller, and Mandler all pointed to the existence of an interpretive memory that is distinct from the more passive forms that psychology had originally studied. The cap on this work came in 1973 when Jean Piaget weighed into the field. Piaget was already widely admired for his research on child development, work that went back to the 1920s. His memory research had certain things in common with those studies. He used children as subjects, and his experiments asked children to work with various bits of physical apparatus. But Piaget's memory experiments did not focus on stages of development. Instead Piaget hoped to gain some understanding of what memory was and how it worked. He used children in these experiments because their different levels of development let him control for the role of understanding in memory.

The most important of Piaget's experiments tested children's memory for causes and effects. In one experiment children manipulated levers attached to matchboxes. Although the arrangement of the levers looked similar, the effects of manipulating them differed. In one case, if children pushed a lever, the matchbox went up. In the other case, when they pushed a lever, the box went down. Five-year-olds saw and mentioned the different motions, but they did not wonder about them. After six months they had a poor memory for the experiment. Seven-year-olds did wonder why the motions differed, but they could not find an answer. Six months later, they too had only vague memories of the experiments. Ten-year-olds, however, could understand the experiment at once, and six months later they could recall at least the general principle of the experiment. Many could describe the experiment in good detail. The major point Piaget uncovered is that memory is not simply descriptive. If it were, there would be no clear reason for five-year-olds to forget so much when ten-year-olds remember so well. After all, five-year-olds do remember many things for more than six months. Instead, memory depends on a capacity to interpret the experience. It is not enough simply to see a peculiarity. To remember we must have some explanation for the peculiarity.

In discussing his findings, Piaget made a remark that can stand as the first principle of interpretive memory: "The organization of mental activity presides over memory." Piaget did not say that the objective organization of events presides over memory. We remember things according to our understanding of what happened, not according to the way something really occurred.

Active Memory

Piaget's principle articulated a point that followers of the Ebbinghaus tradition had seen with growing clarity in their own studies. Even the crudest memory experiments show that we tend to impose a subjective order on recall. The simplest experiment uses a list of words or syllables. One presentation is seldom enough to learn a list, so subjects read the list many times before learning it. Repeated presentation, however, carries a technical problem. If subjects see the list in the same order every time, the order itself becomes a reminder and provides a grammar for the experience. One item leads inevitably to the next. So experimenters mix up the list after each presentation. This way, the arrangement of words stays random, and the experience contains no objective order to help remind the subject of what comes next. Yet memory invents an order. Subjects lump parts of such lists together, even though the lumped words may never have really appeared together. Lumps are groups of words that subjects continue to remember in the same order. Studies show that at first, chance alone accounts for these lumps, but we preserve old lumps as we try to remember the list and we form new lumps with each recital. Soon subjects lump many of the words together, giving the lists a consistent order that far outdistances chance. A person will see a list, perhaps car soon laugh open

and recall it as:

open soon car laugh.

It is a small change, but it foretells greater ones that memory imposes. Some lumps are practically inevitable because nearly everybody associates certain words: black-white, knife-fork, boy-girl, and so forth. If both words from such a pair appear on a list, people tend to recall them together, no matter how they originally appeared on a list.

Although these findings are hardly startling, they have subverted Ebbinghaus's ambition—and that of twentieth-century psychology in general—to account for human behavior by referring only to objective things. Skinner hoped to show that all of these objective things existed in the environment. When he failed, cognitive psychologists tried to show that a combination of objective features of the environment and the information stored in the brain could account for memory. The tendency for memories to acquire a subjective order raises problems for this faith in objective factors. Why does memory reflect subjective characteristics?

Further studies showed that shared associations rather than objective features increase the capacity for recall. One classic study of associated recall presented subjects with lists of fifteen words. Some lists used words with no history of association, words like *mouse, winter,* and *government.* Subjects remembered an average of only 5.5 words from these lists. Other lists used words associated with some secret word not included on the list. A list of words associated with *butterfly* might include *moth, net,* and *cocoon.* Recall for these lists averaged 7.35 words. The unmentioned associate improved recall by almost two words, or nearly 40 percent.

Intriguingly, better order confuses recognition. Recognition research began in 1904. The laboratory work of that era reported that when asked to recall items from a presentation, subjects could recall an average x items, but when tested for recognition, subjects could recognize an average $x + y$ items. This finding matched the popular notion that recognition is easier than recall and that idea endured for over half a century. (Even people with amnesia do better at recognition tests than in recall tests.) During the 1960s, researchers began discovering effective ways to foil laboratory recognition. Originally, recognition tests showed a word like *hippopotamus* and then presented subjects with a pair like *hippopotamus/bicycle*. With such different words, recognition is easy, but suppose we show subjects a pair like *hippopotamus/rhinoceros*. Unless you are an experienced safari hand, these words seem pretty similar in their associations, and recognition becomes more difficult. By the middle 1960s, psychologists had grown so skilled at selecting confusing "filler" items in recognition tests that they had turned the old finding on its head. They could do experiments in which subjects recalled an average x correct items, whereas subjects using recognition averaged $x - y$ correct items.

Recognition becomes especially confused when researchers change the context of a study. The first work that showed how to confuse recognition was so complicated it seemed almost comic, but soon researchers refined their techniques. If experimenters present material in one context and test it in another, recognition always stumbles. This type of confusion eventually led George Mandler to break with the Ebbinghaus tradition and bring the study of recognition into Bartlett's side of the field.

All this research confirms what we saw in the previous chapter. Recall uses order; recognition uses context. It also shows us something about subjectivity. Subjective features apparently depend on context to help people find order. Although the importance of context is well known, it again subverts the notion that only objective factors effect learning. A science of memory must acknowledge the private constructions of the individual mind. At every level of memory we have found this same point. On the first step, emotions motivate even rabbit pups. On the second, reminders recall imaginary perceptions. On the third, interpretation organizes behavior.

Meanwhile, other research found that subjective factors effect perception. An important figure in this research has been Herbert Simon. Based at Pittsburgh's Carnegie-Mellon Institute, Simon is a man of broad interests who has won a Nobel Prize in economics and coauthored the first computer program in artificial intelligence. His other interests include memory and chess. Combining these last two, he began a series of experiments to discover how the memory of a chess master differs from the memory of ordinary chess players.

Chess masters like to astonish amateurs by playing several games simultaneously, while blindfolded. During the mid-1960s, research into the memory of chess masters and that of ordinary chess players found that the differences between them arose from their perceptions. Ordinary players look at a chess board and see mostly individual pieces. They make sense of the situation as they study it, noticing threats and possibilities as they go. Master players perceive groups of pieces as units. For example, they might see three pawns together and think of them as one thing. They understand implicitly many of the unit's dangers and possibilities. When they think about moves, masters think of using these larger units rather than of moving individual pieces. Chess masters can be compared to writers who think in sentences, whereas ordinary chess players are like writers who think one word at a time.

Simon's research into chess-board memory found that when chess masters remember a board they first remember the units and then derive the positions of the individual pieces that comprise the unit. More recent research has established that experts perceive and remember less complicated games like the board game Othello in the same way. It seems likely that experience with almost anything that requires judgment leads to organized perceptions. If we break up units so that the parts are no longer organized in meaningful ways, our capacity to perceive them breaks down. Chess masters are no better than anyone else at remembering positions in which pieces appear randomly placed on the chess board.

To non-chess masters, this perception can sound a little mystical; however, we all perceive some things as units. If I present you with a list of eleven letters for recall

CATMOUSEDOG

you can probably immediately repeat the letters. A non-English speaker, however, would find the task more difficult. Success depends on previous knowledge. Yet anyone who knows the secret of combining the eleven letters does so well that three words probably popped out at him. This quality is a peculiarity of meaningful units. Those in the know perceive them whole. It takes an effort to break them down into their elements. We perceive much of our daily life this way. If we set a table, for example, we do not have to count every utensil to see if each is in place. We look and see it. If a spoon is missing, we simply perceive its absence and know to fetch one. But a person not raised in a knife-and-fork culture could not do so. The perception of these units depends on memory, not on nature. Interpretive memory organizes the present as well as the past, a surprising finding in anybody's book.

Most of these findings about active memory came as a surprise to their discoverers as well. Lumping and reorganizing lists, confused recognition, and perceptual units were uncovered by researchers who were originally wedded more closely to the Ebbinghaus than to the Bartlett tradition of memory. They found consistently that a passive storehouse model of memory cannot explain experimental results that stress the role of grammar and context.

Piaget, of course, was less surprised than others by this research. He is not immune to criticism, but Piaget never mistook the mind for something passive. He summarized this group of findings in interpretive memory's second great principle: "Memory depends on a person's capacity to construct an experience." There is no storehouse or file cabinet where memories are preserved. We construct a memory and remember the construction rather than the original event. When we recall items grouped together, we reorganize them because we have constructed the list in our own way. Some readers might feel more comfortable if the principle said we *reconstruct* an experience instead of saying *construct*. The difference is not quite a quibble. *Reconstruct* preserves the traditional notion that memory follows an objective blueprint hauled out from the files to guide our actions. If we do use a blueprint, however, it is often one that has undergone some heavy tinkering, for what we build usually differs from what we found before. The word *construct* emphasizes the point that memory is an imaginative act that assembles parts into a whole.

One of Piaget's memory experiments showed this construction process particularly clearly. He tested children's recall for a demonstration in which one rolling ball transferred its energy to a second ball, but the second rolling ball could not transfer its energy to a third. The age at which children correctly explained this experiment varied greatly, but most children could think of some explanation for what happened, and they continued to remember something of the experiment, recalling it in ways that emphasized their own explanation. In the demonstration, balls rolled down slopes. One girl mistakenly explained the experiment by saying the third ball did not begin to roll because the slopes grew flatter. The slopes did not flatten as she said, but the girl's drawings depicted a flattening anyway.

Two eight-year-olds in the experiment were puzzled at first by the demonstration, but eventually they figured out the reason for the failure of the energy transfer. The second ball comes to a sudden halt just before it hits the third ball. The early drawings by these two children did not portray the experiment correctly, but after six months they realized the balls must not have touched and they drew the experiment correctly, showing a gap between the second and third balls. Understanding had made their memories better.

This important finding accords with Piaget's second principle, that memory depends on a capacity to construct an experience. Theories that try to explain memory as retrieval from storage deny that such improvement can happen. Of course, it misses the point completely to reply that the children do not remember what they saw, but rely on their better comprehension. Piaget's work shows the interdependence of memory and understanding; the capacity to learn about the present implies a capacity to learn about the past as well. We realize the importance of things we had ignored and suddenly we say to ourselves, "Oh, that is why such-and-such happened," or, "Ah-ha, that is what so-and-so meant."

Memory Chunks

Two decades before Piaget's book, in the early 1950s, George Miller developed a model of memory that accounts exactly for Piaget's principles of interpretive memory. In a small masterpiece of modern psychology titled "The Magical Number Seven, Plus or Minus Two," Miller studied the act of interpreting experience as it occurs and then recalling its details correctly. He called this action "chunking" because subjects grasp chunks of experience. His essay quickly became standard reading in undergraduate psychology classes, and memory scholars commonly include Miller's discovery among the most important in the field of memory studies of the past forty years. Yet, for all the excitement it inspired, the work may have been "premature." Chunking, at first, seemed to many psychologists like a stage act.

To understand chunking, consider an experiment Miller described in which subjects learn to hear and repeat forty binary digits. A binary digit is either a 0 or a 1. Forty binary digits look like

0110010000110101110110000110100110001110.

If you try reading these digits aloud, I think you will see what a baffling experience the numbers present. Yet people can learn to recite them after one hearing.

The subjects of the experiment were not memory freaks or mathematical wonders, but they had received special training in their task. At first, most of them had been able to remember a string of no more than seven digits. Then they learned how to recognize groups of digits. Among mathematicians binary digits form a special number system and have meaning. For example, the pair of digits 01 is equivalent to the single number 1. The subjects in the chunking experiment learned these values for pairs of binary numbers, and remembered their meanings. Thus, in the forty-digit list above, they would remember the first pair not as two digits, but as the number 1. The second pair, 10, could be called by the number two; 00 is read as zero and 11 as 3. These groups of digits are what Miller called a chunk. Each is a meaningful unit that organizes a precise experience. Most people would hear the digits 0 and 1 and treat them as isolated items. But the experimental subjects remembered them as members of a small chunk.

Take another look at the first six digits in that forty-digit string. They are: *011001*. Even this small string is intimidating. Some people cannot recite it correctly after one hearing and those who do remember it correctly usually feel they are coming to the end of their rope. But people trained in chunking hear them in groups: *01 10 01*. Had you noticed before that the last pair matched the first? If you remember these chunks by their meanings, they are 1-2-1.

Now, 121 is an easy string to remember. Almost everybody can recite it after just one hearing and feel he or she could have done more. If you know the secret of chunking, you quickly can reduce the pressure on yourself. Yet forty digits separated into chunk pairs still leave a formidable-sounding string of numbers:

12100311311012212032

None of the subjects in the experiment could remember such a long string of chunks, so they learned how to organize these small chunks into fewer but larger chunks.

This system of forming and combining chunks keeps enlarging the number of digits implicit in a single chunk. The idea is similar to learning to spell long words. If we see the word CAT, we perceive it as a unit. If we see the longer, word, CATER, we see it too is a unit. (Because the *a* in this second word has a different pronunciation, it may even take a moment for a person to notice that it contains a familiar smaller word.) The word CATERPILLAR expands the chunk even further. In fact, this one word contains as many letters as the CATMOUSEDOG string we saw earlier, only that string contained three chunks instead of one.

We could expand the DOG part of that string as well—to DOGMA and then DOGMATICALLY. MOUSE expands to MOUSETRAP. If we put these three words side by side

CATERPILLARMOUSETRAPDOGMATICALLY,

they do not leap out at most people with the same force as the CATMOUSEDOG chunks, but a single scanning of the line serves to discover them. And an adequate speller could immediately repeat a string of thirty-two letters simply by remembering three chunks. If we were to add one eight-letter word to our list, as in

CATERPILLARMOUSETRAPDOGMATICALLYAQUARIUM,

the good spellers among us could recite forty letters after one reading.

By learning to organize binary digits into the equivalent of long words, the subjects Miller described acquired a skill most people had never encountered before, but the idea was the same as reading. We convert strings of meaningless units into meaningful wholes. It is bargain day at the memory market; one memory gets you a bundle.

Eventually subjects using these chunking procedures could derive eight binary digits by remembering one symbol. At this stage a person needed to remember only five chunks to derive forty binary digits. It sounds like a skill that takes more practice and training than it is worth, but the experiment made its point: People with ordinary powers of memory can learn to do things that sound impossible. Furthermore, the training and practice included no effort to improve the subject's storage capacity. Instead, it taught ways to construct what one remembers.

Sometimes people denounce memory skills like these as "tricks" or even "mere tricks." The complaint confounds me. A "trick" is an action that creates the illusion of having done something one has not done. When a pigeon flies from a top hat, we call it a trick because it looks as though the bird materialized from thin air. But what is illusory about recalling those forty digits? Nobody secretly wrote them down. The person really has heard the numbers and repeated them from memory. There is nothing fake or illusory about chunking. It is a common method of interpreting and recalling experience.

"Trick" is also sometimes used as an unflattering synonym for "technique." But chunking is not a typical memory-improving technique either. Chunking is standardized rather than inventive. When chunking binary digits, for example, 01 always means 1. A person does not invent spontaneous and imaginative images or associations to impose meaning on something, like calling 01 "winking eyes."

I suspect that behind this "trick" objection is the old subjectivity-objectivity struggle. Chunking is unabashedly subjective, and anyone who does not call it by a sneering name has to acknowledge the importance of subjective factors to memory. Lurking behind that dispute is the nature of memory itself. If it is objective, it must use stored information; if it is subjective, then every memory can be imaginatively constructed.

Miller's work on chunks provides a formalized specific way to think about the poor memory Bartlett observed in the retelling of stories from alien cultures. An English speaker has no clear way to break the story into established chunks, and soon forgets the original organization and point. Research has clearly established that we remember conventionally organized stories better than unconventionally organized ones, and this tendency does not change with age.

A chunk is a unit of associations whose constituent elements can be derived simply by recalling the chunk. For example, if I say, "I boarded a bus," the single word *boarded* can imply: approached the door, stepped up, paid fare, moved back. But none of those associates need be expressed unless there was some deviation, as in, "I boarded the bus and saw the driver was so busy cursing a trucker that I slipped by without paying a fare." Similarly, if a bore tells you, "To get home from work today I joined a line of riders, waited my turn, stepped up onto the bus, paid my fare, and then went on toward the back," you are likely to recall all of this as simply: He boarded a bus. This chunking is a routine way of understanding and recalling experience.

Chunking is a flexible concept because the constituent elements may themselves be chunks. I might just say, "I rode the bus home today." That chunk of "rode the bus" includes the "boarded the bus" chunk plus a "disembarked" chunk and is ambiguous about a "found a seat" or "had to stand" chunk. Thus, if I recall riding a bus, I automatically know I boarded it and, if need be, can try to recall any details of the experience that might be important. Chunking memories leads to automatic reminders of what else may have happened in an experience. These reminders let us construct a detailed memory.

Notice how chunking uses two separate acts of memory:

- First, the subject must recognize the chunk—he perceives an experience in chunks.
- Second, the subject must recall the contents of the chunk—he derives their contents.

Memory for a chunk requires the cooperation of both recognition and recall. Recognition interprets experience as we perceive it. Recall produces the details of the experience. Every chunk depends on perceptual associations that let us recognize it as a whole and grammatical associations that let us recall its details.

Forever Fallible

Many people find the implications of chunked memory profoundly disturbing. We believe in and want to know the truth. We are used to abundant documentation, to tape recordings and to filmed images. We have many tools for preserving the past, but chunks imply that, at best, our memories can be no better than our insights. When we remember something, our minds do not consult some file cabinet to check a dossier containing a fixed truth. We imagine what happened in the past and then we believe our own construction. As a consequence, we remember things that never happened; we combine memories so that the details of separate incidents become hopelessly intertwined; we remember words, but change their tone; we consistently forget the way we saw things in the past, remembering ourselves as being much the way we are now.

The principle that mental organization presides over memory guarantees that often we will remember the order of events incorrectly. Eyewitnesses may have the details of a crime right but still have the chronology wrong. The police may ask, "Are you sure he mentioned X only after Y mentioned it?" But being sure does not mean a person is right. When describing events, many a person says, "The first thing that happened was _____." Chances are good that something else happened first.

Other people build toward a climax, saying first there was trivial event A, then ordinary event B, followed by interesting event C, and lastly came astounding development D. But in objective reality, matters seldom progress so neatly. These people are not liars, nor do they deliberately use narrative technique to embellish their tales. It is simply that memory is not a tape recorder. People recall experiences in the way they themselves interpret them and are at least as likely to recall their prejudices as their real experiences. This finding impedes the point of memory, which is to cope with the world as it really is instead of accepting old assumptions that may be valid no longer. This principle guarantees that even the best of us will remember many points falsely, and the worst of us will go about smugly claiming fictitious memories that prove our prejudices. We become impervious both to logic and experience, because no matter how the issues fall out, memory recalls them as confirming expectations.

Many people recognize the power of prejudice, and an honest observer may hesitate to insist on a detail that supports a notorious bias, but even if we avoid the big injustices, chunking promises a tendency to recall creations rather than the reality of a thousand details. I have personally experienced this tendency ever since my college days. I introduce myself as "Blair" and am remembered as "Brian." A woman who had forgotten my name recently said to me, "Now, I know your name isn't Brian," but more often people approach and say confidently, "Oh, Brian." I suspect the confusion arises in the first phoneme. Both *l* and *r* are liquid consonants, and many languages confuse the sounds. *Bl* occurs in English phonology, but *Br* is more common; so people who need to remember my strange name can become hopelessly lost if, instead of knowing my name as a single chunk, they try to construct it. How, after that first wrong turn, they arrive unerringly at Brian, I cannot say. I'm just glad they don't recollect me as "Br'er B'ar."

Besides causing us to honestly remember complete fabrications, memory's tendency to lump things together encourages us to invent associations that exist only in the mind and to preserve old associations that no longer exist in reality. Even with the best of intentions, therefore, gossip will often get a story wrong. If someone tries to recall the guests at a party, he is likely to recall customary pairs together even if they were not together, and to invent other couples who have been lumped together only in memory. The careless observer recalls that John and his wife Martha were both at the party, without noticing that he never saw the two speaking to one another. Meanwhile, the same observer concludes that Bill and Jane have become an item, because he saw them talking at some other party. He once lumped them together in memory, and now, come to think of it, saw them both at this latest party. So gossip is perpetually astonished by divorces that "arose from no-where" and continually believes in secret romances that never become public.

Naturally these confusions make people angry and suspicious. If we pulled dossiers from storage, we could look up a detail and see what happened. But construction depends heavily on interpretation and can lead to bitter self-righteous disputes. One person says, "You said X." The other indignantly replies, "I never said anything like that." Although this dispute sounds like a simple fight about memory, it is complicated by the reliance on two functions of memory. One person recalls X; the other person fails to recognize X. Each feels injured, one thinking, "I never," and the other wondering, "How can he deny . . .?" Perhaps if the two could work out the context of the remarks, they could develop a memory they both agreed on and in which neither person felt injured. But passions intrude, and instead of helping matters, fractured memory only convinces both sides they are in the right.

Creative Memory

Yet, for all its fallibility, chunked memories give us an adaptability and flexibility not common to bureaucrats who trust only their files. Interpretive memory matters for exactly the same reason that emotional and factual memory matters. It enables us to cope with the present. It provides a way of growing wiser from experience. Even though it leads to many errors about what happened in the past, interpretive memory is powerful when it comes to figuring out the here and now. Chunking permits us to put our expectations to use. If we know the grammar of an experience, we can interpret an event as it happens, becoming drawn in personally as well as intellectually. The sports fan finds a moment more exciting than the novice, even though the fan can remember one hundred similar incidents while the novice never saw the situation before. Instead of habituating to the familiar scene, the fan is alert to all the possibilities and waits to see what will happen.

Most remarkable of all is interpretive memory's ability to form associations we have never experienced. When applied to the past, this ability can lead to error, but the same capacity allows us to confront the present with a splendid creativity. The most thoroughly studied example of this freedom is in language. It lets us speak things never said before. The simplest examples, however, come from spatial chunking.

Spatial memory begins at the factual level as we learn a sequence of places. Evidence suggests, reasonably enough, that a mammal's spatial memory depends on its foraging requirements. Our own elaborate memory may have first begun to evolve because our ancestors had to remember a complicated three-dimensional space in the treetops of a vast forest.

Insights into spatial memory come when two separate strings of spatial associations merge to form one larger chunk, as happened for me below the Taft Bridge. As with any other chunk, spatial chunks permit creative action. For example, once you have learned a path that leads from tree to hill to home, you could also learn about a separate trail that passes a cave before coming to the hill on the first path. Having learned this second path, you do not only remember two ways to get home. You can also remember how to get from the tree on one path to the cave on the other path.

Here we see the special power that comes from chunking. Emotional and factual memory depend on specific experiences. The context of the experience may go forgotten, leaving only emotional or factual associations, but the memories derive from the episodes of one's life. Chunking permits something new. I have an experience—traveling from tree to home. Even though I may never have had the specific experience of traveling from tree to cave, my spatial chunk lets me know how to get there. At this interpretive level, I can "remember" something I have never done. In normal speech, we do not call this memory "remembering." We feel more comfortable saying a person can "figure out" or "imagine" how to get from the tree to the cave. But chunked associations make the distinction between memory and imagination a vague and uncertain one. From memory's perspective, the distinction is also trivial. Memory needs to cope with the present, and chunked associations permit that.

This finding is probably the greatest surprise of memory research. The difference between memory and thought, a difference that once seemed so clear, has become elusive and obscure. It has become an issue of semantics. When we speak of our knowledge about the past, we shall presumably continue to speak of our memories. When we speak of finding new solutions to problems, we will speak about our imagination. But these different words refer to the nature of the problem, not to the qualities and powers of mind we use. Memory unites with thought at every level of the staircase. The immediate interests and attractions we feel are part of emotional memory. Factual memory gives us the generalized competence that gets us through the routines of the day, and the imaginative figuring that finds new solutions comes from interpretive memory.

Conscious Memory

Having reached the top of the staircase, we perceive the world differently, and we express these changes through our symbols. Language, art, music, and prayer are part of every culture and, given the interpretive nature of our memory, it could not be otherwise. Most of these expressions follow an established grammar and stay with the familiar chunks of the art, but sometimes expressions go beyond tradition and seem to cut more deeply into reality than had previously seemed possible. Piaget's memory research showed the basis for such enrichment. With this final experiment we can see how memory works on the new level it has raised us to.

Piaget showed some children two U-shaped tubes, each containing a fluid. One tube was open at both ends and its fluid rested normally, level in the tube. The second tube, however, had a cork in one end. Air pressure in the open end pushed the liquid against the cork, so the levels of liquid were uneven. In this experiment, Piaget showed the children something they could not understand. Even the twelve-year-olds could not explain the odd water levels in the second tube, but the apparatus was so simple that all the children could easily describe it.

He told the children they would see the apparatus for a short time and then have to draw it from memory. As the children looked at the U-tubes, *none* of them remarked on the peculiarity of the fluid levels in the cork-stopped tube. Only when they considered their own drawings did they begin to wonder about the disparity between the levels in the tubes. One eleven-year-old said, "This level [in the cork-stuffed tube] bothers me because it isn't the same as the other one." Then came a creative association: "It must be the cork." A week later he drew the apparatus again, remembering to show the cork and uneven levels. He said, "I still don't understand it." Interestingly, the boy's explanation was wrong (or at least incomplete), yet his memory was right. Explanations do not have to be right to help memory; they just have to put an experience into a context.

Another boy behaved a bit differently. He first drew the U-tubes with even water levels in the corked tube. Then he felt something was wrong and changed the drawing, correctly showing the levels as uneven. But he had no insight about the cork's role. Most of the children were like this boy. They did not remark on the oddity of the water levels until they made their own drawings. Then they saw that something unusual was afoot and corrected their work to show that peculiarity. Of course, without some insight to preside over their memory, they forgot the details of the experience. Unlike the boy who said, "It must be the cork," most of the children's memories faded. After six months they had forgotten the cork, forgotten the U-tubes, and remembered only the curious difference in liquid levels. Children tended to draw bottles instead of tubes. One bottle contained a normal flat liquid; one held a liquid resting on an odd angle.

In discussing his findings, Piaget articulated a third principle of interpretive memory: "Improvement in memory results from a conflict between recall and recognition." This third experiment shows what he meant. There is a tension between what we perceive and what we construct. With the boy who corrected his original drawing, grammar first misled him. He recalled the second tube as normal, then recognized the error when he looked at his drawing, and made a correction. The recall-recognition discrepancy helped him discover a difference between expectation and experience.

The other boy remembered the equipment correctly, but when he saw his drawing he felt bothered. He recognized the drawing as historically correct and yet failed to recognize it as grammatically possible. He could have reacted dogmatically, saying that his memory must be wrong and "correcting" his drawing to suit his prejudices. Instead, he stood by his drawing, and tried to correct his grammar. The boy did not have enough of an insight to create a new chunk, but his grammar for water levels became irregular. He knew that water usually seeks its own level, but he found that the rule did not hold true in the presence of a cork. The other subjects did not respond so deeply to the conflict that they revised their understanding. They did not associate a context with the irregularity they observed. They underwent the same type of memory decline Bartlett described over fifty years ago. As in the memory for an Indian folk tale, the children's memory for the water levels grew simpler and more banal. Only the crudest hint of the original oddity survived. But when the tension between recall and recognition provokes a new association, memory works well, even though confused.

In interpretive memory, recall and recognition normally support and enrich one another. After insight, for example, recognition of facts suddenly overcomes the fan effect, the tendency of recognition to slow down as we learn more and

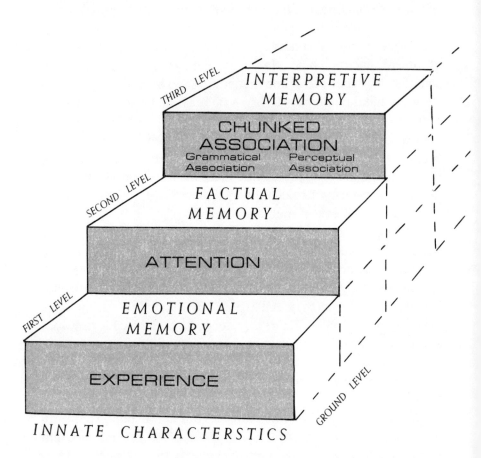

THIRD LEVEL

*INTERPRETIVE
MEMORY*

CHUNKED
ASSOCIATION
Grammatical   Perceptual
Association   Association

SECOND LEVEL

*FACTUAL
MEMORY*

ATTENTION

FIRST LEVEL

*EMOTIONAL
MEMORY*

EXPERIENCE

GROUND LEVEL

INNATE   CHARACTERSTICS

Interpretive Memory: Construction of memory's third step begins when an insight combines a perception and its grammar (the connections between parts) into one chunk. When the step is fully constructed, understanding lifts an organism to the level of conscious behavior. Behavior on this level is called by various other names as well—e.g., purposeful, deliberate, creative.

more facts. Once people interpret facts as part of a larger insight, the effect disappears. Recognition comes more quickly than ever. At this level of expertise, too, people begin saying they recognize many statements that they have never before seen, and they suddenly stop recognizing meaningful statements that they have met before. The new factor is plausibility. If a person's insight makes a supposed fact plausible, that person tends to recognize the "fact" as familiar. For example, a person who discovers a connection between two paths will find that a proposed route between two points on the paths will sound familiar even though he has never traveled that particular route. It sounds plausible to him. We usually recognize facts that outright contradict an insight (although such facts are hard to recall). We would remember the problem if, for some mysterious reason, the route between the path points did not work. But often we cannot recall or recognize a fact that is simply irrelevant to the insight. We see this problem often enough when people discover they have forgotten a short cut. They understand the long route, but that understanding is irrelevant to the short cut, and even though they have gone the short way before, they get lost.

Operation on this third level distinguishes the effects of human memory from those of other creatures. The tension between the recognition of experience and the recall of grammatical organization can lead to consciously formed associations. These irregularities can elaborate on and perhaps ultimately overthrow earlier insights. They have filled the world with tools, art, and meaning. When formalized, this testing between particular experience and general expectation is the scientific method. Artistic tension is less rigorously defined, but more open to surprising and telling associations. The tensions of interpretive memory lie at the center of the artful world we have made for ourselves. Through memory's staircase we have brought ourselves to a new place indeed.

6

THE ARTS OF MEMORY

Though I do not deny that memory can be helped by places and images, yet the best memory is based on three most important things, namely study, order, and care.

—Erasmus, *De ratione studii,* 1512

The ancient distinction between the natural memory we are born with and artificial memory dependent on practiced skills no longer seems quite so sharp. Every memory has a history behind it. We create our memories and we create the ability to use them. The ancient system of artificial memory deliberately created a memory chunk, but each of us builds and uses memory chunks all the time. On the other hand, we can distinguish between the natural and artificial uses of memory. Natural memory has a long evolutionary history, and serves to steer us through the present. It is not concerned with what happened in the past, only with using the past so that we can face the present as expertly as possible. Useful as this ability is, there are times when people want to know exactly what happened. Because nature did not give us the power to preserve old information, people have had to invent it.

We usually think of inventions as visible things, but the artificial memory of the ancients was more like the invention of the curve ball. Nature has given us the ability to throw things, but nature never had to strike out Babe Ruth. It takes discipline, training, and practice to become a pitcher. It also takes more than one pitch. Along with the curve ball a successful pitcher should include in his repertoire a fastball, slider, or perhaps a knuckleball. Similarly, the accurate recall of old information is a special skill that requires more than one technique. The ancients spoke of their method as though it were the only deliberate skill in memory, but there are many arts of memory. Each redirects natural talents toward new purposes, but they rely on different steps in a memory staircase. Each requires discipline as well. Good artificial memories always require hard work.

Civilization builds on details. The more complex the society, the more it must remember. If American society lost its technology for preserving details, it would begin to dissolve within minutes. Today's hottest technology encodes, stores, retrieves, and organizes information, but the need to aid memory predates electronic technology, predates even literacy. Oral traditions tell long stories in verse instead of prose, almost certainly because the rhythm makes verse easier to remember. It may have also helped preliterate poets with their composition. The Argentinian writer Jorge Luis Borges said, "Blindness made me take up the writing of poetry again. Since rough drafts were denied me, I had to fall back on memory. It is obviously easier to remember verse than prose and to remember regular verse forms rather than free ones." Word processors are only the latest refinement in a many-millennia-long drive to find ways to preserve the labors of imagination.

As powerful as the technology of retrieval has become, however, it cannot take over all the details of surviving. In daily experience the most common and annoying memory failure is the forgetting of names. We recognize a face and can almost recall the name that goes with it. But the name does not come. Psychologists call this confusion the "tip of the tongue" phenomenon. Often as you try to recall the name, you can tell what it begins with, but then do not know how to get from that first phoneme to the next. The grammar of the sounds comprising the name is too arbitrary for ready construction. This problem haunts presidential aspirants every four years as they desperately seek ways of making voters remember their names. They traipse through New England snow and Midwestern rain, shrieking like Marley to Scrooge, "Remember me." Then they turn up for thirty seconds on the evening news, speaking of dire matters. "Who's that?" asks one viewer, slightly moved by what he heard. "Oh," says a friend, "you know. That's, uh, oh, ooh, I've got his name on the tip of my tongue," and somebody else goes on to win his party's nomination.

Even recognition can fill us with uncertainty. We commonly meet this problem in restaurants as we try to identify our waiter. Most notorious of all is the tendency to confuse faces of people who belong to racial or ethnic groups different from one's own. A glance that judges "Jew," or "black," or "Mexican" separates a person from the anonymous mass without adding anything meaningful to the observation.

Adding to the confusion, memory refuses to be silent. If we do not know, we do not know, but memory often makes us think we do remember something, even when we do not. If we see a person and sometime later somebody asks, "What color tie did he wear?" we may reply, "Green," and believe ourselves correct, but we may be wrong. Our inventions seldom come out of whole cloth, but with the details that emotion bypasses, the material we habituate to, and the expectations that memory imagines, human narrative memory is distressingly suspect. So we turn to deliberate techniques for improving memory.

Hypnotism

Most artificial systems begin with attention. They use techniques for learning, but sometimes we want to remember what has already happened. The ways of recovering the details of some bygone experience have always tended to be a little spooky, favoring divination, oracles, and omens. And one further mysterious technique has survived. Hypnotism tries to use the power of suggestion to make us remember particular events. When it works, the hypnotist suggests a context for recalling associations.

The nature of hypnosis remains so mysterious that usually we define it in terms of the techniques used to induce it. A hypnotist tells people to relax, to concentrate on some small detail, and to rely on the hypnotist's voice for other details about their experience. The hypnotist begins suggesting experiences to the subject. Usually the first suggestions are real—perhaps pointing out the feel of the watch on one's wrist. But soon the hypnotist suggests experiences that do not exist—perhaps claiming that the room is hot and stuffy—yet the subject responds as though the suggestions were real. A truly hypnotized person does experience the suggestions, hallucinating perceptions as the hypnotist calls them forth. Part of the mystery of hypnosis is the simplicity of the technique used to induce it. A highly hypnotizable person can enter the state quickly and easily, yet the hallucinatory condition that follows seems difficult and profound. One feels that drugs, starvation, or religious ecstasy ought to precede such a thing.

Some sensational police cases have used hypnotism to solve crimes. In the Boston Strangler case of the 1960s, hypnosis provided information that led to physical evidence. In a kidnapping case in Chowchilla, California, a hypnotized witness recalled a license plate number that led to rescue and arrest. Events like these received plenty of publicity and raised public confidence in the use of hypnosis as a desirable police tool. One survey of college students found a nearly unanimous (96 percent) belief that hypnosis could enable people to remember things that would otherwise stay forgotten. But no matter how mysterious the power or sensitive the technique, we cannot break into a mental file cabinet and retrieve a memory. We must construct what we remember.

Two Maryland appeals court rulings bracket the golden age of police hypnosis. In 1968 the court ruled that witnesses could give "hypnotically refreshed" testimony. In 1982 the court reversed itself and forbade such testimony. Between those years the police in many states, not only Maryland, used hypnosis. Sometimes witnesses were even asked to recall events beyond their powers of perception. A witness could be asked to remember a scene through imaginary binoculars and describe people who were too far away for clear vision. An even more radical approach used hypnosis to see the unseeable. A hypnotized witness in a case where robbers wore ski masks might be asked to (imaginatively) rip off the mask and describe the thief's face. Questions like these call for more than refreshed memory. They are attempts to turn witnesses into Clark Kents and ask them to use the perceptual powers found only on the planet Krypton. Interestingly, the witnesses did not reply, "Give me a break." They provided the requested descriptions. The practice of hypnotizing witnesses has not yet completely disappeared, but because of doubts held by most courts, today's use is more cautious. A 1987 ruling by the U.S. Supreme Court left it to individual judges to allow or forbid testimony based on hypnosis.

Piaget said that memory improvements arise from a conflict between recall and recognition. His principle challenges hypnosis at its heart, for hypnosis removes this conflict altogether by replacing recognition with suggestion. A hypnotic state is an increased willingness to perceive suggestions as real. Normally, when recall and recognition work together, the two continually reinforce each other and a person feels by their continued agreement that his memory is correct. When the two no longer agree, a person becomes bothered and either remembers better or says he is not sure. Under hypnosis a person receives continual reinforcement from the hypnotist, who constantly says things like, "Good" or "You're doing fine." When a hypnotist stops saying these things, the subject becomes bothered and begins to elaborate on a memory.

Not surprisingly then, hypnotized memory works best when the hypnotist himself already knows the context and the answer to a question. The hypnotist actively assists in the construction of a memory. One older experiment that reported astonishing memory feats dates back to 1949. A hypnotist found that 93 percent of his subjects could remember what day of the week their tenth birthday had fallen on. Can you do that? Sixty-nine percent of the subjects could even recall the day their fourth birthday fell on. This latter is particularly astonishing since follow-up studies have established that on any given day bright four-year-olds do not know the day of the week. It turns out, however, that the hypnotist knew the answer to his own question before he asked it, and he did not ask, "What day of the week was it?" Instead, he asked, "Was it Monday? . . . Was it Tuesday? . . ." and so on until the subject stopped him. Current opinion holds that the hypnotist unconsciously communicated the answers to subjects, and got those very answers back. Many hypnosis experiments show the same results we often see in experiments into extrasensory perception. As controls grow tighter and the hypnotist himself does not know the answer, the results grow less impressive. Since hypnotism uses suggestion, no one should be startled to learn that when we impede a hypnotist's power to suggest accurately, the subject's ability to recall accurately declines.

When the hypnotist knows many details of an experience, he can ask specific questions and get correct answers. In one experiment subjects saw a movie and were asked detailed questions like, "Immediately after the title of the film was shown, a young man carrying some books was shown walking along in front of several billboards. What was the color of his sports jacket?" Highly hypnotizable subjects got an unusual number of answers right, but the question helped them. All the question's details about the young man, books, and billboards are correct. The question suggests a specific and accurate context.

In real life it is extremely hard to devise detailed questions with sure accuracy. Correct details can establish a specific context and help the subject recall a correct answer, but erroneous details lead subjects to an incorrect context, and that produces error. Experiments indicate that hypnosis ceases to help when subjects must give answers to interviewers who do not know the correct details. Ordinarily, people with bothered memories will say, "I'm not sure," but hypnosis radically alters a person's willingness to express a memory. The subject confabulates, inventing and believing a memory. One classic example tells of a subject who, before entering hypnosis, had been unable to recall the second stanza of Longfellow's poem about the village blacksmith. When hypnotized, however, he rattled off:

> The smithy whistles at his forge
> As he shapes the iron band;
> The smith is very happy
> As he owes not any man.

This sounds plausible, and pretty well captures the quality I expect from Longfellow; however, the actual stanza reads:

> His hair is crisp and black, and long,
> His face is like the tan:
> His brow is wet with honest sweat,
> He earns what e'er he can,
> And looks the whole world in the face,
> For he owes not any man.

Hypnosis had not improved the man's memory, only made him more willing to try something. He did get much of the last line right, yet even there he missed the lead word, and that uncertainty could well be enough to make a normal person hesitant about claiming even to recall the last line. Confabulations like these are the great plague of hypnosis. They make it possible for witnesses to provide an answer when asked to view an incident through imaginary binoculars or to imagine ripping off the mask of a thief. But the answer compounds invention with accurate memory, and no one can hope to sort them out.

Hypnosis has been a hot research topic in memory studies of the 1980s. Generally we find that hypnosis does not work better than the old police technique of going over and over an experience. In the late 1970s experimenters showed that repeated attempts to recall an event eventually lead to much improved memory for an experience.

One notable experiment first used repeated recall to aid subjects in remembering a series of pictures they had seen. Then subjects were hypnotized to try to make them remember still more, but most of the newly recalled pictures were confabulations, especially for highly hypnotizable subjects. Hypnosis, it seems, is no substitute for hard work.

Hypnosis has another serious drawback. People are much more certain about their memory when it is based on hypnosis. The doubts and hesitations that normally trouble a person trying to recall events disappear after one's memory has been "hypnotically refreshed." The issue is particularly important in courtroom testimony, where jurors often pay close attention to how confident a witness seems. Were I a trial lawyer, I would want to hypnotize all my witnesses before facing a jury. Cross-examination will not shake them. But if I were a judge, I would never allow such a witness in my courtroom. The witness's testimony has become tampered evidence and must be considered as suspect as a reconstructed fingerprint. Experiments also show that we can tell a hypnotized person that something imaginary happened in the past, and then, after the hypnotic state, the person will claim to remember such an experience. So if I were an unscrupulous trial lawyer, I could really manipulate my witnesses.

Reminders

Techniques like hypnotism stumble because memory uses the past, but does not preserve it. Over fifty years ago Bartlett concluded that, "Remembering is not the re-excitation of innumerable fixed, lifeless and fragmentary traces. It is an imaginative reconstruction, or construction, built out of the relation of our attitude towards a whole mass of organized past reactions or experience." Everything we have learned since then has confirmed this principle. Successful memory techniques start with this fact of construction and go on from there. Every important memory system begins with factual association. One thing automatically reminds us of another.

Artificial memory systems begin with something easily recalled that reminds us of something harder to recall. This technique is the paradox of memory systems, or mnemonics. They all give us more to remember. People who already feel that their memories are besieged sometimes respond with dismay when they discover that memory systems begin by increasing rather than decreasing what they have to remember. This commonsense criticism always makes skeptics hesitant about bothering to learn a memory system. As one Chinese student said when a sixteenth-century Jesuit missionary tried to teach him artificial memory, "Though the precepts are the true rules of memory, one has to have a remarkably fine memory to make any use of them." But reminders form the basis of all artificial memory.

The simplest reminder uses the cartoon solution of tying a string around one's finger. Remembering to do something at an appointed time is among memory's most difficult challenges. Although memory helps us answer the question of what we must do now, it uses the past to answer the question. Unusual appointments that break with routine have no established associations to help guide our actions, so we often resort to physical reminders. A person can shift his watch to the other arm, thus reminding himself of the appointment whenever he checks the time. Other systems, such as putting something by the door, are even more common.

Another reminder uses mental imagery. Suppose you have to go to a certain store the next day. It is easy to forget that sort of chore. You hop in your car and follow a routine that is so automatic the store never enters your head. To remind yourself, you can imagine the next day's scene, beginning with getting into the car. Conjure up the image as clearly as possible of the dashboard and steering wheel. Imagine placing the key in the ignition and make that action the reminder. Tell yourself: "As I place the key in the ignition I must remember to stop off at the shoe store and pick up my boots." Now imagine the scene again and, as you imagine placing the key in the ignition, think of the boots. It sounds a little mystical, but the system works for many people. It uses two elements of factual memory—reminders and perception.

Modern society emphasizes symbolic thinking, especially thinking in words, but factual memory relives perceptions. I have always thought in words, but since beginning research into memory I have made deliberate use of perceptual associations. Remembering names, for example, has always been a nightmare for me, but I find I can sometimes remember a name by remembering the introduction. I hear a third party's voice say the name aloud and I see the person's face. Of course, this system works only after a formal introduction, a fact that makes me wonder if the widespread problem of learning names partially arises from society's increasing informality.

Although remembering an introduction may sound miraculous, it is in keeping with a common experience of factual memory—the little tune that keeps running through the head. If you can remember the sound of music, you can probably remember the sound of a friend saying, "Albert, I'd like you to meet Victoria."

Remembering an image clearly enough to use it as a reminder may also sound impossible. My own mental imagery has always seemed appallingly bad and many people claim they never think with images. A good test for doubters is to ask them to describe aloud the Taj Mahal. Usually the person interrupts his own description to say, "What do you know. I do think with images."

When artificial memory collapsed as a standard tool of education, the prestige of mental imagery also collapsed. Many people, of course, have continued to think in images and sounds, but it has no cultural endorsement as *the* way to think or even as an important way to think. Good memories, however, depend on an ability to use perceptions (real or imaginary) as reminders.

Rote Memory

Memory systems that require long strings of associations work best when we organize reminders into chunks; however, we can also organize them as a long string in which each item reminds a person of the next one. This system is called rote memorization. School children commonly use it when they must recite a poem or famous piece of oratory:

"Four score . . ."
               automatically reminds a person to say
"and seven years ago . . ."
               which reminds him to say
"our fathers . . ."
               reminding him of
"brought forth on this continent. . . ."

During the classical age of artificial memory, rote memory had little serious standing, but then artificial memory came under attack from several directions. One group objected that artificial memory was too emotional. The English Puritan William Perkins denounced the system in 1592 saying,

> The artificial memory which consists in places and images will teach how to retain notions in memory easily and without labour. But it is not to be approved [because:] The animation of the images which is the key of memory is impious: because it calls up absurd thoughts, insolent, prodigious and the like which stimulate and light up depraved carnal affections.

Perkins favored rote learning. Rote memorization uses the reminders of factual memory but skips their emotional basis. Because rote learning depends on repetition instead of arousal, rote memorization is slow and impeded by wandering interest. For centuries, teachers have justified memorization tasks as a way to improve the students' memories. William James seems to have had such a teacher, and plainly he hated those tasks, for he denounced them with great vigor in his adult life. His classic text, *Psychology,* devotes five pages to castigating the theory that rote memorizing leads to better powers of memory. He even did some experiments that supported his belief that rote memorizing of one thing does not make it easier to learn the next thing. James overstated his case. It is possible to improve one's memory, but none of the techniques used in rote learning help. Rote reminders are too simple and specific to permit much generalized memory improvement.

Generations of rote learning have led to some entrenched ideas about memory. Like the metaphors from the classic system of artificial memory, rote memory's assumptions have been generalized beyond the specific situation that provoked them. Because rote memorization can use only a few items at a time, many people assume we have a fixed memory span, and because memorization requires frequent repetition, much opinion holds that all memory requires rehearsal.

Belief in a memory span acquired support during the very first days of scientific memory study. Ebbinghaus discovered that if he tried to learn a list of seven or fewer syllables, one reading served to do the trick. But if the list grew longer, even one item longer, he needed several readings to learn the list. This seemed like pretty good evidence that the brain might have a limited storage capacity; however, we have seen that several factors affect factual memory. Prompt recall enables us to remember up to four items. If an experience arouses us, we can form many associations, but in this unpredictable system a person may suddenly habituate to an experience and cease learning. The uncertainties of habituation confound attempts to measure the supposed memory span. If we habituate at once, we pay attention to only one item. Adding the four items available through prompt recall gives us a five-item memory span, and this bottom-of-the-memory-span value turns up in many studies. Unless a list has some special structure or unless experimental subjects use some memory-improving technique, people usually recall between five and six items from a list. On the other hand, if we never habituate to an experience there is no reason to assume any upper limit on the memory span.

One means for postponing habituation imposes meaning on an otherwise random experience. Experiments have shown repeatedly that we remember meaningful associations best of all. One careful study investigated several ways of meaningful pairing. Experimenters asked subjects to learn word pairs. They told one group simply to learn them by paying attention. This group's recall average was the standard, bottom-of-the-memory-span value: 5.57.

A second group read the pairs, and then read a sentence linking the two words. For example, a sentence joining a pair like *hat/bucket* might say: "Her hat fell in the bucket." Average recall for these pairs showed a significant improvement: 8.17 items.

A third group of subjects read the word pairs, and then made up their own sentences to link the words. This method added personal reference since, presumably, one's own sentences catch one's spirit better than the sentences made up by an experimenter. Average recall for these subjects was 11.5 items, double the rate for those who tried rote learning.

A final group read the word pairs and formed their own visual images linking the words. To link *hat/bucket,* for example, a person might imagine somebody pouring water from a hat into a bucket. Average recall for this group was 13.1 items. This amount of recall well exceeds normal measures of memory span. Even arbitrary meaning helps memory more than no meaning. Inevitably, artificial memory systems that give meaning to something work better than the reminder strings of rote memory.

Because one experience seldom permits learning every item in a string, rote memorization usually requires rehearsal—the deliberate, continuous repetition of material. Rehearsal forces the creation of a chunk of reminders, and its effects can last a lifetime. Even older people, when asked to recite the alphabet, still say "L-M-N-O" as almost a single word because they learned the letters that way when they were schoolchildren.

Rote memory requires grouping reminders into chunks. If we want to remember a credit card number, for example, it will do us no good to read the whole thing and then try to rehearse it. We must read only a few items and rehearse them before going on. An unfamiliar telephone number is just short enough to permit a unified rehearsal. The seven digits are perfectly dull and meaningless, so habituation comes fast, but with determination we can recall all seven digits while moving from phone book to telephone. Usually we remember such a list through the forced attention of reciting the phone number over and over. The next time we want to call that number, however, we will probably have to look it up again.

Rehearsal has an unfortunate side effect. It alienates a person from the memory. The memory persists but it has been drained of emotion and meaning. Sometimes this power can be therapeutic, as in the terrible case of a friend who saw a man leap to his death in front of an oncoming subway train. For twenty-four hours the scene repeated itself in my friend's mind. It was all he could talk about, all he could think about. His colleagues at work reported he was worthless that day as he sat helplessly with his one memory; however, this incessant rehearsal had a healing quality. By the end of the second day, my friend reported that he had experienced the scene so many times it had lost all meaning and emotion for him.

His experience contains a warning. If rehearsal can have this dissociative effect on something as emotional as the sight of a suicide, we should not be surprised that students using rote rehearsal end by remembering only their alienation. For centuries schools have wasted their pupils' time with a technique that does not improve their general powers of memory. Worse, the technique fosters hatred for its subject matter. It is not right that thirty years after leaving the eighth grade I should still shudder with boredom whenever anyone threatens to recite the Gettysburg Address. Of course, sometimes we do have to learn strings of numbers or lists of names. For small tasks, rote memory can serve, but large assignments need better techniques.

Mnemonics

Instead of practicing meaningless strings of reminders, memory systems work better when we organize the reminders into an easily understood chunk. Memory systems of this type artificially carry us to the level of interpretive memory, but instead of following from an insight, artificial memory imposes an arbitrary grammar on the reminders. This technique is the great secret of artificial memory, discovered, it is said, twenty-five centuries ago by a poet, Simonides of Ceos. He had just left a party when his host's palace collapsed, crushing all the revelers. They did not have dental records in those days, and the bodies were too mangled for ready identification. Simonides, however, remembered where everyone had been sitting, and so could identify each body for burial in the proper family plot. Impressed by his achievement, Simonides then analyzed his memory into two parts—places and images. Using the vocabulary of today's memory studies, we would say that Simonides discovered that memory chunks use grammar and perceptions.

The space (or grammar) in an artificial memory system can use any set of associations that automatically leads from one reminder to the next. In a familiar house, for example, one room automatically connects to another room. An imaginary space can be indefinitely large and, therefore, can contain as many reminders as we need; however, we have more paper than the ancients enjoyed and seldom need to recall such long lists. For short lists, we can use acronyms instead of spaces. HOMES, for example, is a popular acronym for recalling the names of the Great Lakes. (Huron, Ontario, Michigan, Erie, and Superior.) The grammar of an acronym uses spelling rules. If we remember the chunk HOMES, we quickly recall the letters and the associated lakes. We can also use simple sentences to hold reminders. To this day I can still recall the first four hydrocarbons: methane, ethane, propane, and butane. They come to mind at once because a high school classmate tipped me to the sentence: *Mary eats peanut butter*. The first letter of each word in the sentence matches the letter that starts the appropriate chemical name. So if I remember the sentence, I can reconstruct the list. The peanut-butter sentence links my limited knowledge of carbon rings to my better knowledge of English grammar and spelling. From that sure ground I can make associations, confident that I have listed these chemicals in the proper order.

Each of these mnemonic systems works by creating an artificial memory chunk. A chunk always organizes details into a grammatical arrangement. The details are what Simonides called images, but any system of reminders will serve. The chunk's grammar automatically moves a person from one reminder to the next. Once you know this technique, it becomes trivially easy to invent artificial chunks. A woman from my neighborhood tells me she had trouble recalling the arrangement of three main north-south avenues—Columbus, Amsterdam, and Broadway. She needed to find some simple grammar that would automatically remind her of the names in the proper order. Her solution used an acronym. The word *cab* organizes the avenues' initials correctly. She could have picked some other grammatical organization, perhaps a sentence *(Come along, Bill)* or even historical chronology *(Columbus's voyage led to the founding of New Amsterdam, which gave us Broadway)*.

At some point it becomes difficult to remember one's memory aids. It is easy if you have one or two, but if a person has many, it gets harder. This problem led to one of the most famous of the classic rules for artificial memory: Make your aids so bizarre that there is no confusing them. As the *Ad Herennium* put it:

> Now nature herself teaches us what we should do [in selecting reminders]. When we see in every day life things that are petty, ordinary, and banal, we generally fail to remember them, because the mind is not being stirred by anything novel or marvelous. But if we see or hear something exceptionally base, dishonorable, unusual, great, unbelievable, or ridiculous, that we are likely to remember for a long time. . . . Nor could this be so for any other reason than that ordinary things easily

slip from the memory while the striking and novel stay longer in the mind. . . . We ought then to set up images of a kind that can adhere longest in memory. And we shall do so . . . if we set up images that are not many or vague but active; if we assign to them exceptional beauty or singular ugliness; if we ornament some of them, as with crowns or purple cloaks . . . or if we somehow disfigure them, as by introducing one stained with blood or soiled with mud or smeared with red paint, so that its form is more striking, or by assigning certain comic effects to our images, for that, too, will ensure our remembering them more readily.

We can take this advice to heart. For example, if the HOMES acronym is too boring for easy recall you can reorganize the letters into the pseudo-Yiddish insult SHMOE, meaning a jerk, drip, or naive twit. What sort of SHMOE thinks the Great Lakes are filled with lemonade? A bizarre association like that is easier to remember than the ordinary word HOMES. But centuries ago people rebelled against the emptiness of these random associations. If you find yourself creating so many artificial systems that keeping them straight has become a challenge, it is time to regroup. At some point in life we need insightful memory systems.

Cartesian Memory

During the 1930s Gestalt psychologists looked for a better method of learning than rote memory. Their research showed the power of insight. Subjects in one experiment studied the following list for three minutes:

2 9 3 3 3 6 4 0 4 3 4 7
5 8 1 2 1 5 1 9 2 2 2 6

Half the subjects learned the numbers by rote, and they performed routinely. One-third of these rote learners could reproduce the list perfectly immediately after the three minutes, but recall suffered badly after three weeks and no one could give the whole thing. Another half of the subjects studied the numbers and hunted for some organizing rule. At the end of three minutes, 38 percent of this second group could give the numbers, a slight improvement over the rote learning. Even better, 23 percent of the group could still remember the list perfectly after three weeks. The discovery of a rule is easier than rote learning, and the effect lasts longer.[1]

A rule is an automatic procedure for getting from one reminder to another; however, unlike the artificial memory of the ancients, the grammar is not arbitrarily imposed on the reminders. Memory on this level begins with an insight into a chunk's grammar. A person who knows the grammar of a chunk can automatically derive the reminders. At this point we can even "remember" parts of the chunk we have never encountered. We can derive a third line for the Gestalt experimental list

$$5\ 0\ 5\ 4\ 5\ 7\ 6\ 1\ 6\ 4\ 6\ 8$$

even though we did not see the line. At this level, memory systems have acquired the creative powers of interpretive memory.

I call this system of recall Cartesian memory because the philosopher René Descartes first described it as an alternative to the classical artificial memory system. "I thought," wrote the philosopher, "of an easy way of making myself master of all I discovered through the imagination. This would be done through the reduction of things to their causes. Since all can be reduced to one, it is obviously not necessary to remember all the sciences. When one understands the causes all vanished images can easily be found again in the brain through the impression of the cause. This is the true art of memory."

Cartesian memory works by defining the grammar of associations so precisely that we do not need many reminders. We

---

[1]The rule: begin at lower left digit, add 3, add 4, then repeat the addition cycle. This procedure yields 5, 8, 12, 15 . . .

can derive the whole system simply by following the grammar from its starting place. In the Gestalt experiment, if you remember the rule that leads from point to point, you need only to remember to start at 5. Even that final point collapses into part of the rule: Add 3 and 4 and begin at 5. The 3-4-5 sequence is a natural grammar.

Deriving rules, no matter how absurd, is a useful memory system. "I'm at the hotel," says a visitor, "room 680." You reply, "That will be easy to remember because I'm going to arrive at 6 o'clock. There are two other digits in the number, which gives 8, leaving the final number with nothing, or 0. 680." It sounds mad, but it works.

Insight of a more serious kind can also help actors learn their lines without rote memorization. From a performer's perspective, a play has many characteristics of a mnemonic chunk. Things follow in fixed sequence, giving the play a grammar. Each speaking place in a play begins with a reminder, some specific word or action that cues the arrival of a line. The easiest way to learn the words that follow the reminder comes through insight into the emotion and situation of the moment in the play. The cue reminds a performer of the emotion and situation, and the words associated with the cue flow almost naturally. Of course, for this method to work, performers need to understand how their words mesh with the movement of the play. It is axiomatic that a performer who has not yet learned a line has not yet figured out what that line means. To learn his lines, an actor should concentrate on understanding why they are said, not concentrate on rote learning.

Cartesian memory has served us well during the past few centuries and is certain to remain important, but computers can now beat people at Cartesian memory. We can program a computer to follow a rule through a chunk. A simple home computer could derive and print twenty lines of the Gestalt experiment's list while we were writing out just the third line. If Cartesian memory were the apex of all possible memory arts, the invention of the computer would guarantee eventual unemployment for most human thinkers. Computers are simply better than us at preserving information and following rules. Our powers of recall cannot compete forever with their precision and tirelessness, but interpretive memory beats computer operations in two ways. We recognize a chunk's context and we use insight to form new chunks. In the future, the cutting edge of artificial memory will lie in building new chunks and recognizing new contexts for their application.

Technological advances in storing information have always enlarged the demands made on artificial memory. Preliterate societies worked hard just to preserve their own classics. Ancient literate societies wrote down the classics, so people used artificial memory to preserve their own ideas and needs. Cheap paper made the preservation of one's own thoughts easy, so people turned to Cartesian memory to explore the implications of their thoughts more deeply. Now we have computers that can tirelessly and rapidly explore chunks, so today's artificial memory will have to excel at creating new chunks.

PART
TWO

THE BIOLOGY OF
MEMORY

7

NEWFOUND SURPRISES

Unanticipated novelty, the new discovery, can emerge
only to the extent that [someone's] anticipations about
nature and his instruments [for study] prove wrong.

—Thomas Kuhn, *The Structure of Scientific
Revolutions*, 1962

Science has studied memory for over a century, yet
this book could not have appeared even five years ago. Yes,
researchers acquired most of the data about memory's functioning before the 1980s began, but facts make sense only after they
come together in a chunk. The memory chunk came together in
the mid-1980s when research into the nervous system gained
momentum, and the result has not turned out as researchers had
anticipated. The upheaval has overturned a consensus that had
developed in neuroscience laboratories around the nation. Individual scientists, of course, always hold differing theoretical
views, and it may seem to a working scientist that he spends
much of his time disputing ideas, but to an outsider the agreement between scientists is always more striking than their areas
of contention. We see the same thing in ordinary life. Politically
concerned Americans often feel they are in bitter opposition to
other political groups, but a foreign visitor is usually struck by
the enormous agreement between Americans about the importance of private enterprise, public information, and personal
opportunity. To an outside observer, America's political disputes always seem like arguments over points within a consensus. A long-standing consensus also prevailed in the study of the

nervous system; however, in the past few years that agreement has broken.

The Old Consensus

The old consensus held that when the breakthrough in memory studies came, it would explain how the brain files away our memories. By 1980 the storage idea no longer helped explain much of the psychology of memory, but all the metaphors we had about the workings of memory—be they metaphors of wax impressions, art galleries, books, dossiers, phonographs, or computers—all insisted that memories *must be* stored. So scientists expected the breakthrough to tell them how the brain stores memories. Instead, they have discovered how it is possible to remember without storing any information about the past.

A second expectation took it for granted that a breakthrough would resolve which of the various psychological "approaches" to memory studies was right, or at least nearest to the mark. Skinner, Ebbinghaus, and Bartlett began their research with different axioms. They disagreed bitterly about the nature of learning, behavior, and the mind. Other sciences have distinct branches and issues, but none of them has such basic disputes over what to study, what to ask, and how to explain what you observe. Skinner denied the existence of memory. Ebbinghaus said memory existed and was passive. Bartlett said it was active. A real breakthrough, people imagined, would settle the matter about which approach was right. Instead of naming a winning side, however, the breakthrough in neuroscience's memory research has transformed the separate psychological approaches into branches of one larger field.

We live today at the great sunrise of brain knowledge. Centuries of research into the obscurity of brain anatomy and function can at last give other fields of study a context for what they observe. Psychologists have long understood that the causes of their observations lay in the brain, yet most psychologists paid no attention to the question of how the brain works. They knew so little about the brain's operation that there seemed no point in saddling themselves with a series of uncertain and vague propositions. The reverse was also true: Neuroscientists did not linger over psychology even though they understood that psychologists study the effects of brain activity. The grand effects of learning, perceiving, and feeling were too complex for analysis into distinct brain operations. So the two studies went their own ways, until recently. In this section, we shall consider work that has brought the two fields together. The successful combination of psychology and neuroscience promises to become as important to the history of science as Kepler's union of physics and astronomy, Darwin and Wallace's marriage of geology to natural history, or Watson and Crick's fusion of chemistry with genetics.

The dream of a coherent neuropsychology seemed distant for most of this century. A pioneering researcher eager to link the studies was Karl Lashley. He wondered how the brain made learning possible, and he investigated the question from the 1920s through the 1950s. In the end, he offered a despairing joke: "I sometimes feel, in reviewing the evidence on the localization of the memory trace, that the necessary conclusion is that learning just is not possible." Lashley's search for memory's "localization," of course, reflected the assumption taken from artificial memory's method of *loci* that memory sits in a place.

When Lashley began his research he took it for granted that the brain stored its memories somewhere, and he asked where exactly that somewhere lay. He taught rats to run mazes, and then began systematically destroying different sites in the brain to see where the memory was stored. To his surprise, he found that no single place contained the maze. Instead, a rat's ability to run the maze declined in proportion to the total amount of brain destroyed. If a rat suffered much brain damage, the rat retained little maze-running ability; little brain damage left much better performance.

The Lashley experiments proved the falsity of the old portrait of memory as a warehouse, but people hesitated to dismiss the whole memory-storage metaphor. If it is not storage, what is it? Experimental studies of memory's storage grew increasingly like the nineteenth century's study of the aether that supposedly surrounded the earth. Test results became ever more ambiguous and confusing, but physicists could not imagine that the aether did not exist. Today, of course, hardly anybody remembers the aether or what logic required that it be out there in space.

The insistent search for a place of storage has not come simply from a stubborn clinging to assumptions about memory. Everybody could see there was a problem, but beyond the issue of storage lies a conviction that science studies passive things. Most nonscientific societies believe that everything is alive. Rocks, rivers, and the sky, they say, are active living participants in the world. The ancient Greeks thought, for example, that falling rocks accelerate because they are in a hurry to reach a natural resting place on the ground. The scientific revolution changed that attitude. Newton explained the world in terms of an environment that manipulates dead things. His laws of motion describe the motions of the dead—motion based on inertia and external forces. His explanation for the acceleration of a falling rock relies on gravity, an external force that affects the quick and the dead with equal authority. In the centuries since Newton, passive laws have done so well that many people have come to assume that a scientific explanation for something must inevitably describe only the objective environment and never cite any subjective properties. In brain studies this assumption requires that, prior to its being remembered, a memory must already exist in the environment, just waiting to be retrieved. Instead, we find that each memory is a construction, something newly created each time it appears. Memory is actively produced by living things; it is not something passive that a machine can retrieve.

The problems facing the study of memory and the brain in the 1950s matched the difficulties that faced the study of memory and behavior. In behavioral studies, the view of passive memory was giving way to a view of an active constructive memory. Scientists like Miller and Mandler could express this new view without seeming mystical because they assumed that eventually brain studies would show that the brain works like a computer. They expected to learn that what looks like creativity really uses stored memories. Brain research, however, was not having the anticipated success at finding the stored information. Neuroscience had come to a crisis, perhaps the most important of its history.

Searching for a Memory Warehouse

In the late 1960s a psychiatrist at the New York Medical College, Dr. E. Roy John, published a pivotal book entitled *The Mechanisms of Memory*. In it he tried to state the best argument possible for the view that passive, external realities could explain the behavior of the living brain. John suggested that memory is stored, but stored statistically throughout most of the brain. Statistical storage means that the information emerges from the operation of many neurons, as in a democratic vote. John proposed that neurons cast votes and that remembering is a process of discovering how the neurons voted. Changes in a neuron effect its vote and learning is a process of changing the way individual neurons vote. It works like a political campaign. Changing one voter's mind does not matter. A candidate needs a ground swell that changes many votes.

As John knew, the biggest challenge to his position lay in the rising belief that particular brain functions were localized. In the 1950s, as confidence in the notion of stored memories declined, neuroscientists began to suspect that functions of memory were localized. This idea gained strength after 1953, when surgeons performed an experimental brain operation on a patient called H. M. It ended catastrophically, leaving H. M. in a permanent state of amnesia. He no longer learned any new facts. We will examine H. M. in more detail later on. At this point in our story we need only understand that H. M.'s surgery was accepted as conclusive evidence that the destruction of small parts of the brain can have enduring consequences for memory.

This notion of localized functions suggests an active brain that creates its own behavior. Instead of working like a one-neuron one-vote election, the brain becomes a team. Imagine a baseball game in which a ball is hit against the centerfield fence. An outfielder grabs the ball and throws it toward the infield. The second baseman catches the ball and throws it on toward home plate. The shortstop intercepts the ball in midflight and throws toward third, letting a run score, but the third baseman tags out a runner. In this situation too, the result emerges from the activity of a group, but the action is cooperative rather than statistical. Each player has constructed a part of the outcome, and each acted on his own experience, ability, and relation to the situation. If any player had botched his part in the play, the whole system would have failed.

For twenty years now, the basic questions about brain and memory have been the ones John raised. Does the brain's information emerge statistically from the working of its neurons? Or must we understand the brain's activity in terms of localized functions? John's idea of statistically defined information has caused a great stir among mathematicians. By the mid 1980s mathematical conferences regularly included papers about "neural nets" and the statistical information that can emerge from them. This work may show the way to a radical new design for computers. Neuroscience, however, has been less able to absorb John's ideas, largely because of the growing identification of brain areas with specialized functions. The continuing success of this identification has made it increasingly difficult to believe that the brain stores information statistically. It would be an odd baseball game in which a team kept voting about the action of individual players.

The failure to discover a statistical storage system returned the old consensus to the crisis it has faced ever since Lashley proved that the brain has no storage area of the sort found in information-processing machines. In the context of traditional neuroscience, rejecting the storage idea would be as radical as it would be for an American politician to announce that he had concluded that citizens should never gain any information about public affairs. Thus, the continued failure to discover a means of storage is not taken as easy evidence that there is no storage. According to the old consensus, the means of storage simply has not been found yet; however, there is no longer much agreement on the likely nature of the storage.

One popular idea suggests that the information is distributed among the different functional brain areas that neuroscience keeps identifying. In this view memory for different parts of an activity lies scattered about the brain, like bread crumbs through Hansel and Gretel's forest. Each crumb has a specific location, but only the destruction of many crumbs destroys the full memory for the behavior.

Another suggestion proposes that the brain stores every memory everywhere in the brain. The favored metaphor for this omnipresence comes from Karl Pribram, a distinguished neuropsychologist, and former student of Lashley's who likens memory to a hologram. A hologram is a photographic image that stores all its information at every point in the hologram. If part of a hologram is damaged, therefore, the entire image can still be recovered. Although most neuroscientists remain unconvinced, this proposal suggests that some of the finest thinkers in the field believe that only a very bold hypothesis can point the way to the means of storage.

Until recently, surveys of memory usually halted their story at this point. They acknowledged that scientists still do not know how memory is stored, and there ended their brief consideration of memory's biological basis. Tune in for more insight after the missing store is discovered.

Some speculative authors did try to describe in a general way how this storage must work. The most widely discussed

such model was one proposed in 1968 by two cognitive psychologists, Richard Atkinson and Richard Schiffrin. They proposed
three storage areas: a long-term area where memories can lie for
many years before retrieval, a short-term storage area where
memories are held briefly before passing on to the long-term
store, and a vestibule storage point where sensory data first
arrives in the brain. The model's greatest strength is that it
suggests a reason for the poor accuracy of our recall—much
information is lost before reaching long-term storage. Its greatest weakness is that nothing in the brain comes close to looking
as if it could support such a system. Models like the Atkinson-
Schiffrin design appeal more to mathematicians than biologists.
The embarrassing truth is that what we do know about the brain
and its functional areas in no way supports our logical expectations about the storage areas that must be there.

The crisis in the biology of memory continued through the
1970s. In the middle 1980s, however, it suddenly seemed over.
A new consensus had emerged around two principles, and
Lashley's assumption of localized memories no longer seemed
so inevitable. In the final chapter of this section we will discuss
those principles and where inquiries into the biological basis of
memory stand today. But first we will examine the work of two
different researchers whose work illustrates the thinking behind
an emerging new consensus.

8

THE ORGAN OF MEMORY

We need a new vocabulary term to identify such errors—
a nasty word like "mechanomorphism," for example—or
some other way of referring to our thoughtless and super-
stitious habit of attributing mechanical traits to organ-
isms.

—Vicki Hearne, *Adam's Task,* 1986

This chapter reports a key discovery about the biology of memory: The basic nerve cell, the neuron, can make
different responses to identical inputs. One time a chemical from
a neighboring neuron will inhibit an action. Later, the same
chemical will not inhibit the action. It is as though the neuron
itself has learned something. This unexpected finding startled
almost every expert. They had assumed that the neuron worked,
essentially, like a mechanical part in a machine. As recently as
1982, C. D. Woody's authoritative book about memory at the
cellular and chemical level *(Memory, Learning, and Higher
Function)* listed the changes in a neuron that could conceivably
affect memory. The list considered a variety of structural
changes, but it never anticipated the discovery that a neuron
might simply change its responses.

If an automobile control, say the gas pedal, changed its
behavior and began to act like a brake, drivers would complain
and mechanics would scratch their heads. Machinery does not

work that way, and if it did cars would be too dangerous to use. The neuron, however, does work like that: sometimes responding to the world in one way, sometimes another. Its behavior, therefore, does not depend solely on present inputs—the causes that control mechanical behavior—but on past experience as well. It was axiomatic in the old consensus that the neuron is the tool, or perhaps a component, of memory, and that when many neurons work together, learning somehow emerges. Instead it seems the neuron itself is the organ of memory.

No one predicted the astonishing simplicity of these findings. Biologists had confidently expected that something as grand and mysterious as memory would be complicated and intricate. The storage alone would be enormously difficult—all that encoding, preservation, and retrieval. But as we shall see memory uses no storage; the neuron merely begins to behave in a new way. The neuron does not learn in the way that we have always understood learning. It gets no feedback about its behavior and does not seek to enhance its own pleasure or avoid pain. But the neuron does change its actions in response to its history, and of course, if the organ of memory acts as though it were learning, the whole organism will also act as though it has learned.

The Neuron

The neuron is not the only cell type in the human nervous system, nor even the most plentiful type, but it is the primal nerve cell. Sea anemones and sea snails, for example, have nervous systems composed purely of neurons. The neuron first appeared at that evolutionary level, giving a new adaptive power to animal life. The neuron's most obvious specialized characteristic is its use of an electric charge. When properly stimulated, an electric pulse moves across the length of the neuron. The pulse triggers the neuron to emit chemicals, and the great speed of electricity lets the neuron act much more rapidly than it could through ordinary cellular chemical communications.

The discovery of the neuron's electric charge led many to assume that the nervous system was a form of electric wiring and that the body was an electrical machine. The nervous system, however, is not completely electric. The electric charges remain within an individual neuron. A small gap, called a synapse, lies between two neurons, and chemicals, not electricity, cross this gap. Scientists once speculated that electricity arced its way across the synapse, just as it leaps across the gap in an automobile's spark plug. Research in the 1940s led by the British neuroscientist John Eccles refuted this notion. Chemicals, a few molecules at a time, cross the synapse. Chemicals constitute the basic input and output of a neuron. It is the individual neuron, not the brain, that is an electrical device.

Instead of thinking of the nervous system as electrical wiring, we come closer when we use the analogy of a network of computers. Imagine a room like the space launch headquarters at Cape Canaveral, a room filled with computers. Between two computers sits a shared in/out box. The out box of one computer serves as the in box of its neighbor. The computer takes its input, processes it electrically, and then drops its output into the box. The neighbor then takes that output, processes it, and puts any further output into its own box. For rocket launches, it seems practical to have a gaggle of experts, each with his own computer, monitoring and presiding over a rocket lift-off; however, it seems like one hell of a way to design a doorbell.

Indeed, writers often compare the most basic neuron system to a doorbell. If you touch a single neuron at the sea anemone's mouth, it fires, stimulating a muscle. As with a doorbell, when you touch one end of the neuron, the other end fires. It is not quite a doorbell, of course; if you continue poking the neuron, it eventually habituates to the action and stops responding. Doorbells never habituate to being rung. If a pesky salesman keeps pressing a doorbell, the bell will not grow tired and ignore the man's finger. But a sea anemone will do exactly that. It ignores the touch.

With the hindsight of further knowledge about neuron function, we can see that habituation is a telling and remarkable power. Habituation means that the anemone's neuron no longer responds to the same stimulus in the same way. It is a standard part of every level of memory's staircase, so common that we pay it little thought or wonder, especially when it occurs on the neuron level.

The difference comes from the synapse. The all-electric doorbell has no synapse. A charge flows from button to bell without interruption. The sea anemone is different. Press the neuron and you may continue to get electric pulses, but the output into the synapse changes. To return to the analogy of the computer network, the neuron acts like a computer with a changed program.

Imagine a NASA-controlled doorbell. Even at the space program, we need only one computer to run a doorbell. A qualified engineer sits at the computer watching its monitor. The screen shows an input

BUTTON   PUSHED

and then an output

BELL   RUNG.

As he works for NASA, the engineer might have confirmation over a loudspeaker: "Doorbell control speaking. We have bell ring. Repeat, we have achieved bell ring."

As time passes, however, the console keeps showing the same BUTTON PUSHED input and BELL RING output. A salesman has come to vend his wares, and he won't take "Nobody's home" for an answer. Eventually the engineer makes a decision. He changes the ring-bell program for a no-ring program. The console continues to show the BUTTON PUSHED input, but now there is no output.

This space-age doorbell is as automatic as the more familiar variety. The expert monitoring the screen never adds some input of his own, but by changing the program he has altered the system's behavior. The neuron's special powers all reflect this one peculiar ability to change its own programming. Of course a neuron has no NASA-trained expert monitoring its operation. Experience changes its programming.

Freud's Expectations

We had not imagined that neurons could program themselves. For at least a century, the best scientific opinion held that experience does not change the functional part of the nervous system. In a letter to his friend Wilhelm Fliess, Freud specifically stated that the neurons themselves "retain no trace of what has happened." And Freud's early colleague, Joseph Breuer, elaborated on Freud's point in a joint volume he wrote with Freud about hysteria. He argued that the perceptual apparatus must return to its original condition "with the greatest possible rapidity." Yet memory, he noted, depends on change. No single organ can both change and stay the same, so memory must lie outside the functional system. In this view, experience is something to be gotten over. We use it, but we should not be changed by it.

The organization described by the founders of psychoanalysis has become a commonplace of modern technology's information-processing systems. In the 1890s the new phonograph machines offered the best example of such devices. The functional mechanisms in record players are the needle, the loudspeaker, and the wiring that connects the two. This equipment should respond as accurately as possible to its input, but not be permanently changed by that input. We want phonographs that can play Beethoven and then play Chuck Berry without manifesting any lingering effects of Beethoven's music. So we store the music on records and keep them separate from the sound-making part of the system.

This same principle applies even to the most modern computers. We store all data outside the processing system. Processing changes the data; the processor itself never changes. This difference is the source of all those confusing distinctions computer experts make between hardware and software. The hardware does not change; the software does. Manufacturers of high-technology hardware put their electric circuits in silicon chips because of the need for physical stability. Silicon is an element commonly found in sand. It can change its electric charge extremely quickly, showing no undesired long-term effects from its experience with previous electric charges. Silicon does what Breuer assumed the neuron must do, changing its state in fractions of a second.

The logic of these metaphors led Lashley to assume that the brain had a single and separate storage area outside the functional circuits that lead from perception to action. When he proved that no such area existed, he assumed that memory must somehow cache data about experiences throughout the brain. The old consensus agreed that memory is stored somewhere, but not in the neuron. So where is it stored? If you suspect that storage is generally distributed, the most obvious candidate for a storehouse is the synapse. Synapses lie outside the neuron, and yet can influence the neuron's activity. A synapse could make lasting changes in the input received by a neuron, and yet the neuron itself could remain as stable as a switch on a silicon chip.

Logical as the hypothesis of synaptic storage is, it ran into a problem. During the 1970s evidence mounted in many laboratories that neurons change frequently. Surprise over the neuron's puzzling instability was matched by wonder over a strange stability at the synapse. It turns out that the synapse is the most stable part of the neuron network. Synapses do change, but all observed changes are short-lived. Yet the neurons in the human brain change continuously and never return to some "normal" state.

This research was summarized in 1982 in a book titled *The Chemistry of Behavior*. Its authors, Stanislav Reinis and Jerome Goldman, included a remark that showed how far mainstream thinking had strayed from the old consensus:

> In the central nervous system, each of the component neurons . . . differs from all the others by its . . . function, and in particular, previous history. . . .

The old consensus had had no room for talk of a neuron's history, just as today there is no need to discuss the history of a particular location on a computer chip unless we are talking about wear and tear. Previously, any author would have said that neurons differ through their information. This time, however, there could be no differentiation on that point because the authors also wrote, "No such thing as a single locus for each bit of memory exists."

The team metaphor on neuron action was gaining respectability. The brain really might be a team with billions of players, each with its own function and experience. Memory might result from the interactions of team members, but before the might-bes could become likelihoods, somebody somewhere was going to have to show what such teamwork was like.

Alkon's Research

The neuron networks in the human brain are much too complicated for anyone yet to study in detail. We do not know, and probably never can know, the complete neuron-to-neuron activity behind the simplest brain-controlled action. To overcome these difficulties, it is easier to study the simpler nervous systems of sea snails. Their neurons are large and few, and their nervous system does not vary from one individual to another. Yet sea snails are more complicated than sea anemones. Instead of working like an on/off switch, sea-snail neurons can both excite and inhibit action. Some sea snail neurons also synapse with other neurons. In humans, of course, most neurons (99.9997 percent) synapse with other neurons. Several investigators have studied a sea snail's ability to learn. The snails, as you may imagine, have poor memories. At best, they can form short-term sensory associations. Yet sea-snail studies, especially the work of Daniel Alkon at the Marine Biological Laboratory at Wood's Hole on Cape Cod, have proven surprisingly useful for exposing some general principles that underlie the biology of memory.

Normally, sea snails of the species *hermissenda crassicornis* orient themselves toward the light, but if the water becomes too rough they grab on to something to avoid the danger of thrashing seas. This behavior requires two senses, one for light and one to detect water motion. The simplest way to control this behavior would use a two-neuron system. One neuron would be an "eye" that responds to light by triggering an action. The other neuron could veto the motor action whenever the water became too rough. As we are considering a sea creature, we can call this second neuron the admiral. The admiral would sense motion and whenever it did so, it would send inhibitory signals to the eye neuron, preventing it from firing. This two-neuron system would lead to beautifully consistent behavior. Light by itself leads to action; water motion inhibits action. The two-neuron system has no place for memory, and the sea snail's behavior would be purely reflexive. Figure 8-1 illustrates the simple logic behind this two-cell system.

It turns out, however, that the sea snail uses three neurons. It has an "eye" neuron that works exactly as expected. When it detects light, it stimulates a motor action. The sea snail also has a second neuron, which, as expected, can veto the "eye's" signal and inhibit its firing; however, instead of sensing water motion, this second neuron also senses light. When the second neuron detects light, it fires, inhibiting the action of the first neuron.

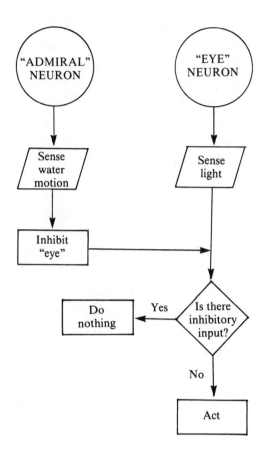

Fig. 8-1. A Two-neuron Reflex: The "admiral" inhibits the "eye" if there is water motion.

It seems peculiar. Two neurons, both sensitive to the same light, both fire when they see light, but one neuron inhibits the other. What is the point? Would it not be easier to stay still without any neurons and without so much effort?

The solution to this puzzle comes from the third neuron in

the system, the predicted admiral neuron. It also works as expected, but in reverse. When the admiral fires, the snail can move. The admiral synapses with the override neuron and continually inhibits its firing. This three-neuron mechanism has a bit of the Rube Goldberg touch to it, but it works. Light appears and the eye neuron begins to fire. The admiral inhibits the override neuron, so the eye neuron does fire and the snail moves toward the light. Only when the admiral detects water motion does it permit the override neuron to fire and veto action. On those occasions, the snail stays still and rides out the stormy sea.

Figure 8-2 illustrates the logic supporting this three-cell system. The final outcome is the same as for the two-cell system. The main change is that the introduction of an override to mediate between admiral and "eye" inverts the logic of the admiral's system. We can see at a glance that this system's logic is less elegant, and practically speaking there are other problems too. A third neuron increases energy consumption and is one more thing that can go wrong.

Evolution has tolerated this seemingly clumsy system because of the effect of experience on the snail's behavior. The override neuron changes the system from a reflex to a memory that uses experience. Alkon has found that the override neuron will sometimes ignore the admiral's veto. This mutiny happens when experience repeatedly associates light with moving water. If a silent admiral neuron repeatedly lets the override fire, the chemical balance within the override neuron changes. It becomes more difficult for the admiral to inhibit the override neuron. Now, no matter what the admiral does, the appearance of light is enough for the override neuron to fire and inhibit's the eye neuron. Input (light plus the admiral's inhibitor) that had previously blocked output now leads to output. In time the override neuron will change again and will accept inhibitions from the admiral, but for the moment it ignores the input. The logic behind this new behavior is shown in Figure 8-3. The

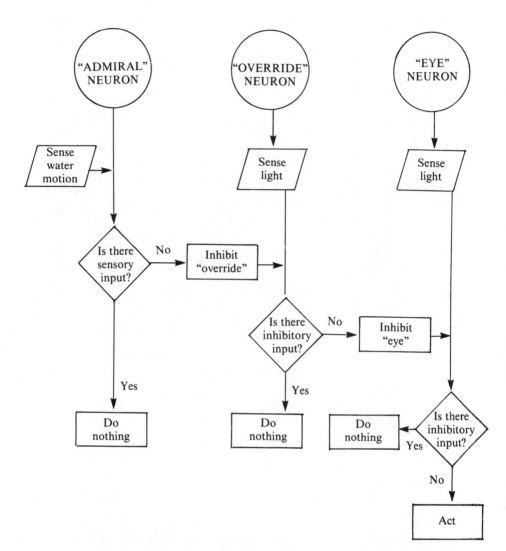

Fig. 8-2. A Three-neuron Reflex: An "override" neuron between the "admiral" and the "eye" complicates the process but leads to the same result as the two-neuron reflex.

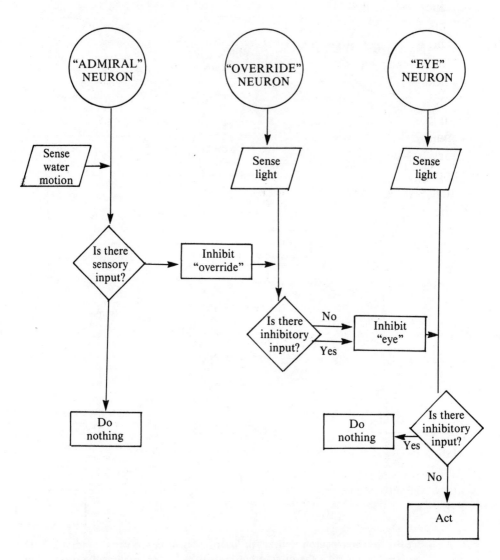

Fig. 8-3. A Three-neuron Memory: By changing its response to identical inputs, the "override" neuron changes the behavior of the system.

illustration matches Figure 8-2, except that now the admiral's input does not matter.

This change helps the snail adapt to the uncertainties of life. The best tactic after rough waters is probably to hang on tight for a while, even when the waters seem calm. Fate being the fickle thing she is, just as the snail starts to move, a wind gust may start the waters sloshing about again. So the third neuron gives memory to the sea snail; it changes the behavior of the snail to suit recent experience. Please take careful note: Memory in the sea snail does not preserve any data; it changes behavior.

Just to deepen the grave for the old consensus, the important chemical changes within the snail's override neuron do not occur at the synapse. They take place near it, but not at it. That detail is secondary, however, to the main point. Alkon has found a way that the nervous system can learn from past experience without storing any information about that experience.

The Engram

At last we have seen a neural team in action. Just as a shortstop may or may not cut off a throw, the snail's override neuron can treat its input in two distinct ways. The term Karl Lashley used for these teams, or fundamental units of memory, was the *engram*. He first imagined the engram as being like a bead stored somewhere in the brain. When that idea proved wrong, he thought bits of the engram might lie scattered about. Whatever the functional unit of memory turns out to be, the term has stuck, and neuropsychologists have determined to call it an engram.

Alkon has shown us a working engram composed of three neurons. Despite the enormous gulf between human and sea-snail memories, Alkon's engram bears some surprising resemblances to what we saw in Part One about the way our own memory functions. Most obviously, the sea snail's memory focuses on present needs instead of on past events. Alkon's engram permits a snail to behave prudently after a storm, but the snail has no recollection of anything about the storm or even that there ever was a storm.

A second recognizable feature of Alkon's engram is its independence. The engram presides over the snail's behavior and needs no central control to direct the neuron's changes. Each neuron acts according to its own experience and only the actions of neurons within the engram determine behavior. The great implications of this independence are summed up in the fact that it takes two charts to describe the logical behavior of these neurons. In even the most complex computer program one chart will serve. We can predict the operation of a machine if we know only its logic and its inputs. In sea snails we need to know history as well. Logic and objective input, of course, matter to the engram's function, but experience is equally important. At last, on a chemical level, we see the introduction of context to the story of behavior.

The sea snail's engram breaks down if we destroy even one of its neurons. The three neurons interact, and depending on which neuron is destroyed, the engram will either never permit motion again or never again let the action of the sea inhibit its motion. The behavior becomes reflexive instead of adaptive.

Nature, however, is seldom so cavalier about the dangers of injury that it lets survival hang by one unprotected thread. In the sea snail's case, it guards against the risk of injury by including several identical engrams in the snail's eyestalk. If one neuron fails, other neurons in other engrams can carry on the work by themselves. This repetition of engrams makes the risks of injury less certain. If we damage the eyestalk, the effect on behavior will depend on the amount of damage. A little destruction will impair performance only a little. Massive damage to the eyestalk will have more serious effects. This proportional damage-to-effect ratio matches exactly with the one that Karl Lashley observed in his experiments with mice. Lashley's results, therefore, need not imply that he had slowly destroyed the stored contents of a single engram. He had killed the functioning of many engrams.

At this point Alkon's three-neuron engram can no longer help us. Alkon studied the operation of one engram with one function. Human behavior, even at its most primitive, is more complex. Yet we can now see that something is localized after all. We do not store data, but the engrams do occupy particular places and damage to those places must damage the accomplishment of their functions.

In older days, we should have expected a long digestive pause to follow Alkon's portrait of a simple engram. Its lack of storage, independence from programming, flexibility, and functional unity have filled a large platter. During that pause conservative defenders of the old consensus about memory could have regrouped, insisting loudly that we cannot draw conclusions about human memory from sea-snail engrams. But our age moves too quickly. In the same year (1984) that Alkon published the monumental summary of his study of the sea snail, a scientist named Magda Arnold published a book describing the location of functions in the human brain. Her work takes us across the giant gap between Alkon's one engram and memory's high staircase.

9

MEMORY CIRCUITS

Only damn plan sounds like grab whatever they can get
their damn hands on . . .

—William Gaddis, *JR*, 1975

Neuropsychology studies brain functions and the circuits that link distinct functional areas. For many years research concentrated on identifying function, but during the 1980s success at identifying circuits has accelerated. This exciting work lets us see how separate parts of the brain can cooperate to construct a memory.

The findings tell us much about the everyday interactions of memory and mind. We can see why conversations fly off on tangents of memory and why we can concentrate for hours on some tasks, remembering what to do as the need arises. The work is exciting, too, because the circuits have no fixed bounds. These loops take away control of behavior from environmental circumstances and hand it to us. Our memories, tastes, emotions, and understanding are critical to the course of the circuits. The brain is not a piece of clockwork that holds us in orbits determined by the mathematics of our situation. It is a biological wonder that lets us use and build on experience, if we dare. The memory circuits have no absolute end. They are loops, leading back to their starting place, letting us move up and down the levels of memory until we ourselves feel that we have remembered enough.

Naturally, the neurons along the circuit are more intricate and complex than those of a sea snail, yet our neurons remain only neurons. The sea snail's neuron changed its internal programming through temporary changes in its chemistry. Neurons in the human brain can undergo many more complex and enduring chemical changes, enabling us to make more subtle and lasting responses to experience. So great is the complex pattern of inputs and outputs in the brain that scientists have yet to identify all the links of a single human neuron. Even so, the many developments in human neurons are only elaborations on the sea snail's neuron. Human neurons can change in more ways, output more things, and interact with more cells. Not surprisingly, therefore, we can do a universe of things impossible for a snail. Yet the basic power of the neuron persists. It can still change its response to unchanged inputs. It remains the organ of memory and serves as the elementary part of the circuit. The brain then transforms this elemental wonder into something still more potent and remarkable, providing us with the powers we need to use the memory staircase. The brain makes the associations and gives the awareness, emotions, attention, and insights that let us use experience to advantage. Thanks to the brain, we become what we experience.

What the Brain Is

The human brain is the most complicated structure in the known universe. Beside it the organization of galaxies, a DNA helix, and even the Pentagon seem like toys of childish simplicity. In this account I will keep the story simple and give only the barest outline of the brain's structure. A brain contains over one trillion cells of different types. Most of these cells are so small that if you saw 100,000 sitting together on a table you would likely assume they were a morsel of dust. It takes several million cells to form a part of the brain large enough to be noticed by the unaided eye. Many bumps, bulges, and twists in the brain have been identified over the centuries by anatomists who had no idea what function they served. Thus, a structure might be called the *pons,* Latin for bridge, because it looked to someone like a bridge. I will refer to structures by their anatomical names only if they are crucial to the story of memory.

Adding to the brain's complexity is its double nature. The body commonly gives us two copies of a crucial organ. We have two eyes, two lungs, and two kidneys. We almost have two brains. The brain is not a ball, but a ball that has mostly been cut in two. The halves are joined by several thick fibrous connectors, but generally the two work independently of one another.

To keep the story as simple as possible, I will describe each circuit as a single thing. The fact that there is, for example, one circuit for emotional memory in the right half of the brain and another in the left half becomes important in memory studies only if part of a circuit is damaged. Then the circuit on the other half may do double duty, just as a person who loses a kidney finds that he can make do with one.

Popular accounts of the brain often stress the existence of these two halves. We read about right- and left-brained tasks, and it is probably true that part of the circuitry for certain highly specialized functions lies mainly in one or the other half. But such specialization comes only at memory's most advanced functioning. In this chapter we are not concerned with the details of particular circuits, but only with their outlines. We want to know how the brain's organization makes possible the memory functions described in Part One, and for that question we can consider one circuit in just one of the brain's halves.

Finally, the brain's complexity reflects its enormously long evolutionary history. Our memory powers are among evolution's most recent developments, and I will not have much to say about the brain's oldest structures. Most of the memory circuitry lies in the most recently evolved region of the brain, known as the cortex. The cortex is the outer part of the brain and includes the scrambled-egg like material we see in photographs and models of the brain. The circuits we understand in the greatest detail handle perception. Perception itself occurs in two separate cortical areas known as sensory and association

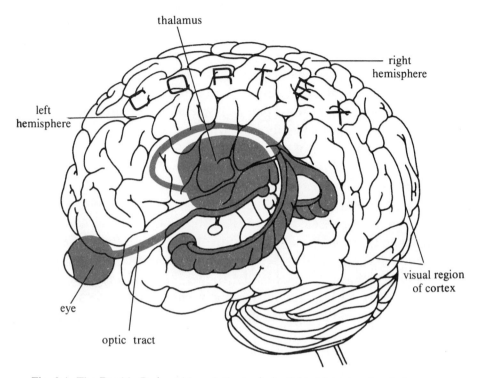

Fig. 9-1. The Double Brain: Although the brain is divided into two hemispheres, its circuits usually operate independently in the separate halves. For example, sight in the left hemisphere begins with stimulation of the eyeball, which excites the optic tract. Input then arrives at the thalamus and from there it travels to the part of the cortex that specializes in vision. An identical circuit lies in the right hemisphere.

cortex. The term *association* reflects an old speculation that this tissue is the site of sensory associations, but we have no evidence to support that idea. For simplicity's sake I will refer to both of these types of cortex by the term *perceptual cortex.*

What the Brain Does

Traditionally, neuroscience imagined the nervous system as simply a mediator between sensory stimulation and motor ac tion; however, this definition has proven too passive. Most obviously, it does not take into account such self-generated actions as getting up from a desk and preparing a cup of coffee. Nothing has happened out in the environment to account for this self-willed behavior. The nesting activities of birds are common natural examples of creatures actively responding to internal urges instead of passively mediating environmental inputs. The brain makes us actors on the world stage instead of serving as just part of the scenery.

Alkon's work has shown that even the simplest nervous systems place an action in the context of memory. The brain lets us benefit from past experience. In every nervous system we see three phases: (1) A *trigger* (stimulation or internal drive) leads to (2) *memory,* which (3) provokes appropriate *action.* The action is appropriate to the memory, not necessarily to the objective characteristics of the trigger. In this chapter we will focus on what happens during the memory phase of an experience. The simplest way to imagine the organization of an experience uses a flow chart. The basic chart for any experience shows:

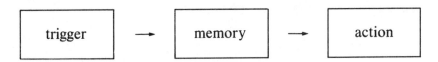

The nervous system controls all three of these stages. In simpler animals we find the stages organized together. The snail's eyestalk contains a complete trigger-memory-action system. As we move up the evolutionary ladder, the nervous system grows more specialized. Sensory stimulation occurs in specific organs like the eyes, ears, and taste buds. Action depends on muscles. And memory occurs in the brain.

The brain brings all our sensory stimulations into one organ, where they can associate and become part of a unified experience—as when a violinist reads a score, listens to his performance, moves his hands, and obeys the conductor all at the same time. Theorizers once argued that all these separate inputs must come together into a single neuron for processing. If the brain worked liked a computer, it would indeed have to bring all inputs into one common processor; however, brain circuits permit a coordination impossible in computers. The circuits permit separate areas of the brain to work together.

The sharpest proof of our ability to coordinate different brain areas has come from the so-called split-brain patients. The split-brain operation, a means of controlling epilepsy, severs the fibers that link the two halves of the brain. The brain is not completely cut in two. Sensory signals still reach both halves, but the brain can no longer communicate between its halves. Cooperation becomes impossible. In everyday life, this operation produces surprisingly few problems, and patients compensate well. Experiments, however, find some subtle difficulties. The leading expert in this field has been Michael Gazzaniga, an American psychologist who has worked with several split-brain patients and written the book *The Bisected Brain*. Gazzaniga's experiments have firmly established that normal behavior depends on an ability to coordinate separate functions. One experiment presents a split-brain patient with a simple two-piece cutout and asks the patient to assemble the pieces. It is the world's easiest jigsaw puzzle. When told to use only one hand, patients can solve the puzzle. Because control of each hand depends on a different half of the brain, we can see that the operation has not damaged either half's visual or hand-control region. But if the patient is told to use both hands, he cannot do it. Coordination of the two hands requires cooperation between two different regions of the brain, and these regions can no longer interact. Coordination is a major brain activity, and brain damage often produces the peculiar effects that come from damaged coordination.

The memory circuits coordinate different functions of memory to give us a unified experience. We, of course, are not aware of experience as bits and pieces. It comes to us whole.

My open mention of awareness, by the way, reflects another development in brain research. Awareness was once a forbidden topic in both psychology and neuroscience. The taboo arose partly because no one can observe it directly and partly because experimental psychology began in reaction against the introspective psychology that studied only awareness. The subject has returned to respectability in recent years, however, because we can observe its effects. We do not know how it happens, but the brain transforms the colors we see, the sounds we hear, and the tastes we savor into a private experience.

The transformation of sensation into perception changes seeing into observing, or hearing to listening, touching to feeling, tasting to savoring. Perception implies stimulation plus something more. In quest of defining that "more" discussions of perception can wander toward mirages, trying to resolve such hopeless questions as whether the red I experience matches the color red you experience. We do better if we stick to the notion that perception combines an unsharable subjective experience with an observable effect on behavior like coming to attention or acting with recognition. If we try to discuss the unsharable experience, we stray from science. We cannot know what a yellow banana looks like to a chimpanzee. But we can discuss attention, acting with recognition, and the brain circuits.

The perceptual circuits we know in richest detail support vision, and within the visual region of the perceptual cortex lie several maps of the retina, the place in the eye where an image first forms. A "map" on the cortex is a region of precise echoing of a stimulation. Visual maps make point-by-point responses to stimulation on the retina. If a small light shines on different points in the retina, corresponding points on the brain's visual maps respond. The maps distort the retina's shape a bit. They put greater emphasis on the details in the center of the eye than on the edges. When we move our eyes to look directly at something, we bring the full power of our visual maps into play. Different maps serve different visual functions. One map is for depth perception, another for color perception, and yet another seems to map complex hand motions. We think some monkeys have as many as fifteen visual maps, and presumably people have at least that many.

The term *map* helps us understand the point-by-point cor-respondence between an image on the retina and an echo in the brain; however, it is a confusing term in one important respect. A map implies a display of information and a reader of the map. Nobody lives in our head reading these maps. They are part of the brain's circuitry. A perceptual map is a functional area of the brain, and can best be understood as a member of the team that constructs an experience. When an eye doctor shines a light on a patient's retina and particular points on the different visual maps respond, it is as though a ball had been put into play. It was caught by the retina and then thrown to particular team members farther on. Of course the complexity of the brain and the many maps soon overwhelm this sports analogy. Different neurons in different functional areas respond to the doctor's light. They catch the throw and (maybe) pass it on. Soon balls are flying about all over the brain, just because of a pinpoint of light. The complexity of the response to so simple a stimulus is terrifying. Yet the basic idea is crucial. The different functional regions work individually and yet cooperatively.

Perception does not simply reproduce; it judges the real world. The best-known example of this power occurs at the movie theater. A moving picture consists, objectively speaking, of a long strip of still pictures. Each picture appears briefly on the screen, to be replaced by another. It is a rapid-fire slide show, but we perceive motion. The movement we see happens in our heads, not on the screen. The importance of this differ-ence becomes apparent if we try to program a computer to watch a movie. A computer has a hard time discovering the motion that we observe automatically. A machine would have to analyze each image in detail, then compare that analysis with an analysis of the previous image, then apply a series of rules to deduce what, if any, movement is underway, and it would have to do this analysis at the rate of twenty-four images per second. Today's fastest super computer could not do it.

Recognition is another function of perception. The memory circuits we will examine show that recognition always occurs on the perceptual cortex. Past perception makes recognition easier, no matter what the condition of circuits in other parts of the brain. We can see these effects best in brain-damaged patients who can no longer learn the associations of factual memory. In one study, patients looked at partial images or words. If they could not identify the item, they saw more of its details until finally they could recognize it. Because the subjects all had amnesia, they promptly forgot about the tests. Without factual memory, they formed no new associations with the images, and the next time they saw the text items they had no recollection of ever having seen them before. But when the experimenters repeated the test, the patients needed fewer details before they could recognize what they saw. Their normal visual cortex was enough to improve recognition.

This creation of experience is, from the perspective of memory studies, what the brain does. The associated inputs of stimuli and the coordinated outputs of behavior depend on this intermediary organ. The richer the experience, the more of the brain we use. Neurons by themselves can give an animal some memory. The brain provides us with a specialized organ for using and experiencing that memory much more profoundly.

Arnold's Circuits

In the past few years we have begun to understand the links between the parts of memory's neuron network. The most comprehensive theoretical work in this field comes from the American neuropsychologist Magda Arnold. Arnold was born in a part of the Austro-Hungarian empire that later became Czechoslovakia. An Old World background often is a part of the Bartlett tradition's leading proponents, and despite her interest in the brain Arnold never ignored the importance of subjective causes for behavior, particularly emotion. Her earlier work includes a two-volume study titled *Emotion and Personality*. She also undertook an important comprehensive study of the way brain damage affects memory, and in 1984, when she was more than eighty years old, she published a full statement of her work in her book *Memory and the Brain*. Hers is the most comprehensive account yet devised of the coordinated memory operations in the brain. Arnold continues the Bartlett tradition of studying memory in the context of personal meaning, imagination, and construction, but instead of testing for memory of stories or of experimental apparatus, she has studied the failures of memory that follow specific forms of brain damage. Her theory organizes these details into a series of memory circuits. Thanks to her work, we at last have a picture of the coordinated actions of different areas of the brain. Arnold describes several loops that comprise the various circuits that lead to memory. Each of these loops move through the brain, and damage to a portion of the loop results in characteristic damage to a person's ability to build a memory.

Arnold's circuits show the relation between several regions of the brain. The first region is the perceptual cortex, and we have already seen that its functional maps operate in complex coordination. A second area of great importance is the limbic system. This region of the brain is, in terms of evolutionary history, much older than the perceptual cortex. A few decades ago scientists sometimes called the region the "nose-brain" because they thought it served only the sense of smell and the emotions that accompany it. Others called it the "crocodile brain," in reference to its ancient evolutionary origins. In Arnold's circuits, the limbic system evaluates a perception's personal importance, so I will call it the evaluation system.

In Arnold's theory, memory circuits cycle through these perception and evaluation areas. The basic route goes from perceptual cortex to evaluation system. This simple two-step function lies behind the many complex associations and levels of human memory. First we perceive something, then we evaluate it. Using the trigger-memory-action flow chart, we can diagram the basic memory this way:

MEMORY

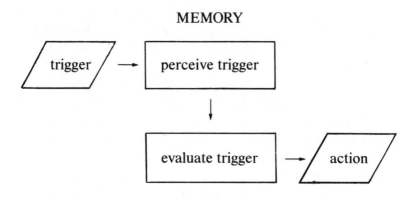

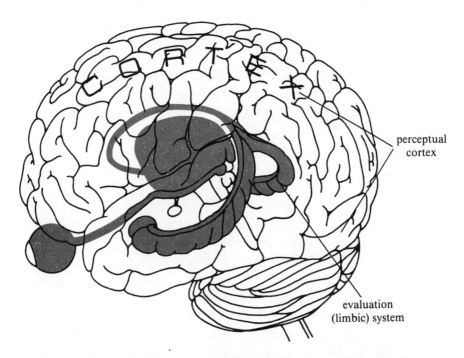

Fig. 9-2. Basic Memory Areas: Memory circuits begin in two cortical regions at the back of the brain—sensory and association cortex, where perception occurs. The brain evaluates perceptions in the structures deep in the brain that comprise the limbic system. This book uses functional names for these areas: *perceptual cortex* and the *evaluation system*.

This system is much less complicated than it would be if we stored our memories. In that case we would first sense the trigger and then look it up in memory to find out what it was.

The Circuit for Emotional Memory

In Part One we saw that emotional memory develops when the perception of an object evokes an emotional response. It is this level of memory that behaviorist experiments focus on. In Arnold's theory, the effects of this level arise from what she called the affective circuit. This circuit begins with the basic perception-evaluation circuit and then loops back on itself.

Much animal memory functions on this level, but it carries a great problem. A creature can become trapped in a situation without evident solution. In these circumstances the circuit may not discover what to do. Memory becomes a trap. Suppose someone does not know an appropriate action, but remembers that the situation leads to pain. We can diagram the problem this way.

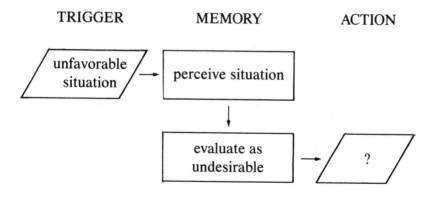

Because the person does not know how to solve the problem, the trigger persists. This cycle of unfavorable circumstance without solution can quickly lead to panic or depression, neither of which helps survival.

Emotional memory can reduce panic by cycling back on itself before turning to action. The emotional circuit normally leads from the evaluation system to a structure known as the hippocampus. The name of this critical organ means sea horse and refers to its shape, which does resemble a sea horse, especially its curly tail. The hippocampus can convert an emotional evaluation into an action, or it can direct the memory to circle back to the evaluation system for further work. This return route follows a million-fiber cable called the fornix to a group of nutlike kernels called the anterior thalamic nuclei. From there the circuit returns to the evaluation system. This route is known to anatomists as the Papez Circuit.

We can see the importance of emotional memory's return route by comparing two experiments with cats. In both experiments, the cats must remember to push a lever. In one experiment, pushing the lever produces milk. This leads to a basic emotional circuit:

TRIGGER   MEMORY   ACTION

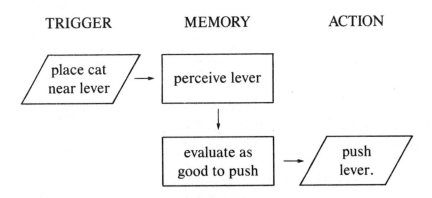

This circuitry works without the cat's ever deliberately saying to itself, "If I push that lever, I can get some milk." Proustian recognition is enough to make it want to push the lever. We know the cat's emotional circuit is simple because destruction

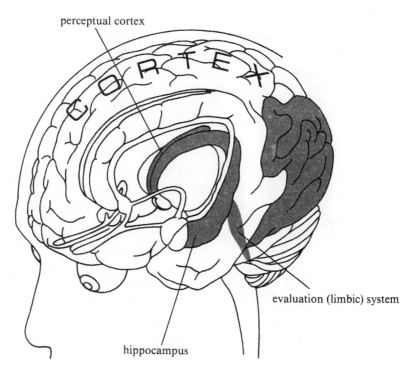

perceptual cortex

evaluation (limbic) system

hippocampus

Fig. 9-3. Emotional Memory's Circuit: Stimulation of the perceptual cortex produces perceptions and then the circuit enters the evaluation system. After evaluation, the circuit travels to the hippocampus, which either signals for action or directs the circuit via the Papez Circuit back to the evaluation system.

of the anterior thalamic nuclei in the return route has no effect on a cat's learning to press the lever. Instead of returning for further evaluation, the hippocampus calls for prompt action. For this most basic memory, a circuit is unnecessary; one input and one emotion is all it takes. But the world does not always make survival so simple.

In another experiment life gets more complicated. Experimenters placed a cat in a box where it received electric shocks. The memory circuit here becomes:

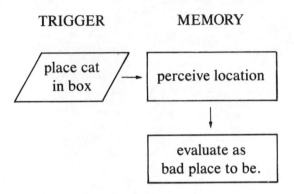

TRIGGER   MEMORY

But what action can the cat take? Normally, the cat would run or jump away, but it is trapped in a box. The solution is to push a lever, so the circuitry must return for a fuller evaluation of the perception. The full logic for the memory stage of the experience says:

MEMORY

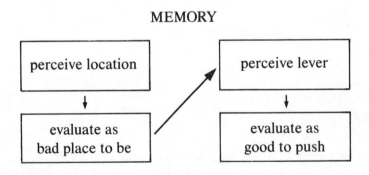

This second evaluation makes sense only in the context of the first one. The cat can learn to push the lever only after it first remembers the unfavorable associations of the setting, and then it must avoid blinding panic. The hippocampus must delay calling for action and direct the circuit back through its return route for further evaluation. We know that such learning requires another lap through the emotional-memory circuit because if we damage the return route the cat cannot learn to press the lever.

Here we see the power that comes by adding a circuit to memory. Neurons do not need brains to change their actions and brains do not need circuits to form associations, but circuits let us put sequences of dependent details into one memory. In theory at least, the emotional circuit could go into a perpetual loop of perception and evaluation, richer perception and evaluation, still richer perception and evaluation . . .

In practice, panic, depression, or something else will put an end to this loop, but the circuit shows that creatures who delay panic can find rich uses for emotional memory even without recalling the reasons for their various emotions. Perhaps people, when caught up in a rich aesthetic experience, cycle endlessly through this circuit. The use of a circuit that can continuously turn back onto itself provides a means for exploring every experience deeply.

The Circuit for Factual Memory

Factual memory, as described in Part One, associates things. One thing reminds a person of another. It is at this level that people learn the arbitrary associations behind classical conditioning and the lists of nonsense syllables that Ebbinghaus studied. Arnold's theory explains this memory by a recall circuit.

The recall circuit sends the neural activity back to the perceptual cortex. Both recall and immediate perception occur at the same perceptual-cortex neurons. If I close my eyes and see again the white cliffs of Dover, my brain re-creates the experience on the visual cortex. Many years ago, when I first crossed the English Channel, I saw those cliffs because light reflected off the land and entered my eyes. That event led to neural action in the visual cortex. Now once again I can see the cliffs and even feel the motion of the ferry as it approaches the land. The energy for the original sight came from the sun, but as I see those cliffs again there is no sunlight bouncing into my eyes. I can revive that awareness because of a circuit that leads away from the evaluation system, back into the perceptual cortex. This reactivation of the same cells explains how I can reexperience the white cliffs of Dover without storing their image in some filing cabinet. I do not retrieve the image from a warehouse; I re-perceive it.

Stimulation of the same perceptual neurons lets us use imagination to remember things. We can subjectively stimulate the same parts of the perceptual cortex that objects in the external world stimulate. The energy that supports such re-perception is less intense, less focused, and less enduring than the energy from first-hand experience. It is unusual for an imaginary perception to be as clear and rich as a perception of something real. But we do perceive anew.

The crucial brain structure in this circuit is the thalamus, a word from the Greek meaning chamber. It serves as the entrance chamber to the perceptual cortex. All sensory organs, except for that of smell, enter the cortex via the thalamus. Neuroscientists have long known that the thalamus is also active during memory. Arnold's circuits explain why. The thalamus is an entrance chamber with many doors. Entrants can arrive from the sense organs or from elsewhere in the brain. Not everything we perceive has come from the outside world.

A complete factual memory adds recall to the circuitry of perception and evaluation. Suppose, as in classical conditioning, we learn to associate a bell with the arrival of food and the association becomes so convincing that our mouths water when we hear the bell. The recall circuit sends our imagination back to perceptual cortex and stimulates an imaginary perception for us to evaluate:

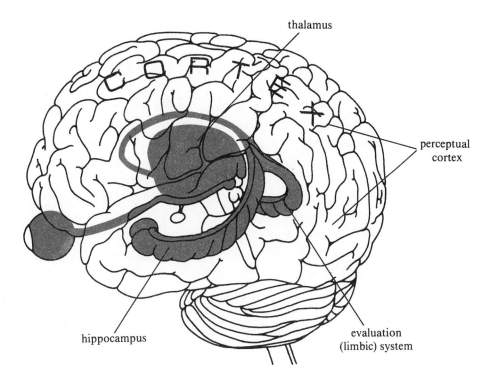

Fig. 9-4. Factual Memory's Circuit: Factual memory's distinguishing characteristic is the recall of a perception. As usual, stimulation of the perceptual cortex excites the evaluation system. The circuit continues to the hippocampus, which directs it toward the thalamus. The thalamus redirects the circuit onto the perceptual cortex, starting the loop again.

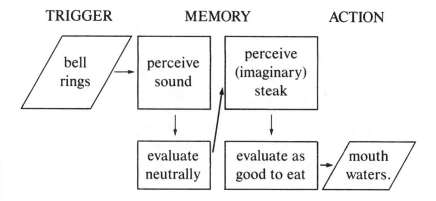

Structurally, this factual memory appears much like the complex emotional memory of the cat in the shock box. The difference is that the second perception is imaginary. Emotional memory can respond only to sensory perceptions; factual memory can create its own perceptions.

The circuit in this system begins like the emotional memory's circuit: Sensations stimulate the perceptual cortex and the evaluation judges the perception. The evaluation, however, does not produce an immediate emotional response. In the presence of a more neutral evaluation, the hippocampus responds by exciting the thalamus, and a new imaginary perception then arises on the perceptual cortex. The circuit has returned to its starting point and the evaluation system judges this new, imaginary, perception. That route, returning to the perceptual cortex for recall of an associated experience, is the basic circuit for factual memory.

The role of the hippocampus in this circuit contributes to learning, but once learned past associations can be remembered without help from the hippocampus. In Chapter 7 we saw the tragic case of an epilepsy patient called H. M. who developed amnesia after radical brain surgery. The surgeons destroyed the hippocampus on both halves of his brain. Naturally, no one ever tried this radical therapy on another human, but researchers have studied many laboratory animals this way. At first it seemed that destruction of the hippocampus had no damaging effects on an animal's memory, but most animal behavior depends on basic emotional memory and the hippocampus does not participate significantly on that level of memory. Closer examination has shown that an animal without a hippocampus does lose factual memory.

It cannot, for example, habituate to new situations. We saw that factual memory begins with an orientation response, which quickly leads to new behavior or habituation. But with a destroyed factual memory, an experience always seems new. An animal never learns about a new trigger and continues to react with an orientation response. Such a damaged animal also cannot unlearn established factual memories, so previously learned behaviors do not become extinct. For example, a cat may learn to press a blue button to open the door into a feeding area. If researchers then destroy the cat's hippocampus, it will continue to press the blue button. Suppose, however, researchers change the situation. Pressing the blue button no longer opens the door. Now the cat must press a red button. Normal cats will learn to ignore the blue in favor of the red button, but a cat with a destroyed hippocampus does not learn. It faithfully continues to press the blue. Even if it accidentally presses the red and opens the door, it does not learn from the accident and continues to push the blue. It can no longer adapt to a changing world.

The hippocampus is critical for the formation of factual associations, but established associations can survive without the hippocampus. Patient H. M. can recall events up to three weeks before his surgery, but he cannot remember anything that has happened more recently. This observation strongly suggests that the hippocampus somehow regulates the development and fine-tuning of memory's circuitry. Once established, the circuits endure by themselves.

The Circuit for Interpretive Memory

Memory's top level combines two separate associations into a chunk. At this level we recognize the meaning of something and construct its details because we understand the chunk. In Arnold's theory these chunks are organized by an imagination circuit.

When neural activity first reaches the evaluative system, the brain can appraise the activity in any of three ways: emotionally, neutrally, or quizzically. An emotional evaluation leads to memory on the level of the emotional circuit. A neutral evaluation directs the circuit toward the hippocampus where it may continue on for factual recall. Sometimes, however, the evaluation system is unable to appraise the perception. In those cases it directs the circuit to the amygdala, another organ in the brain where crucial circuitry begins. The amygdala is important to attention. When researchers destroy the amygdala, the initial arousal of the orientation reaction persists, but the organism no longer focuses its attention. The amygdala can activate neurons along several circuits, and when faced with a puzzling perception it "kicks the matter upstairs" by directing the circuit toward the frontal cortex, one of several areas of the brain specialized for motor behavior. The oldest portion, called the cerebellum, handles motor responses below the level of interpretive memory, like mouth-watering. The frontal cortex controls advanced motor actions.

The frontal cortex gets its name from its presence in the front of the head. This part of the brain gained general notoriety from the surgical frontal lobotomies that sometimes left patients with permanent and severe impairments. Cortex is the most recent evolutionary development in the brain, and the frontal cortex is the most recently evolved cortex. Over the past million years evolution has greatly increased the amount of the human frontal cortex, encouraging people to assume that the cortex is the seat of pure thought. The conclusion seems natural to a society that assumes abstract reasoning is our greatest power, but in fact the frontal cortex governs purposeful action, including the purposeful constructions that govern interpretive memory.

The frontal cortex focuses on the ends of behavior. When I bite into a carrot or say, "Bah, humbug," I may begin with the same mouth action, but their purposes differ so much that separate regions of cortex govern them. This pattern matches our own awareness. When we act voluntarily, we consider the purpose we hope to achieve rather than the muscles to flex. We have little practical knowledge of how we act. Our behavior depends on the coordination of muscles and nerves, but most people have no idea how their muscles work or where they are or which ones help what action. Suppose my right hand rests against my chest and I decide to touch my nose with it. Control

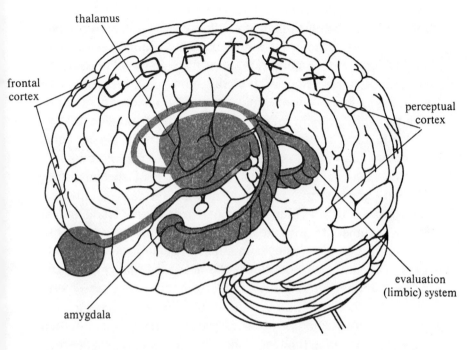

thalamus

frontal
cortex

perceptual
cortex

evaluation
(limbic) system

amygdala

Fig. 9-5. Interpretive Memory's Circuit: The perceptual cortex stimulates the evaluation system, which responds quizzically and directs the circuit to the amygdala. The amygdala kicks the problem upstairs to the frontal cortex. From there the circuit can return via the thalamus back to the perceptual cortex.

of that voluntary action begins in the frontal cortex. Suppose my right hand is on top of my head and again I move to touch my nose. The muscle actions needed to do this second maneuver differ from those of the first, yet both actions begin at the same point in the frontal cortex. Intentional behavior focuses on outcome (touching the nose). Damage to the frontal cortex can impair our ability to act purposefully, and without control over purpose we loose adaptability.

The most subtle form of human adaptability occurs in symbolic expression. We saw an example of this in the insight that let a three-year-old boy break down a phrase and say, "Wait for it to dry," instead of his usual "Wait for it to cool." This insightful deviation from an established motor pattern typifies frontal lobe accomplishments. It allows us to introduce novel deviations into established motor patterns. Some people with damaged interpretive memories suffer from an inability to act as they wish. A person may want to say something, recognize that his speech is inappropriate, and yet still be unable to speak as he wants. This problem follows damage to the frontal cortex.

A standard clinical test known as the Wisconsin card-sorting test shows how bizarre this inability to match actions to understanding can be. The test uses a stack of special cards, each marked by form, color, and number. A card might have three red stars or one blue star or two green triangles. The test requires a subject to sort the cards without knowing whether to sort them by color, shape, or number. The subject, of course, begins randomly. He puts down the first card and then places the second either on top of the first or next to it. The tester says whether the sorting action is right or not. This clue is a big help, and soon almost anybody discovers that the proper method sorts by color. Once the tester sees that the subject has learned to sort by color, he changes the rules. Now he says, "Right," for sorting by form. Normal people quickly realize that the rules have changed, and they begin to search for the new rule.

People with a damaged frontal cortex often cannot act on this rule change. They have not lost the ability to understand the way the world has changed, but their understanding does not improve their behavior. They continue to sort by color although each error brings the news that the action was wrong. Such a peculiar inability to learn anew seems like some grotesque breakdown of the imagination. The patient appears unable to benefit from endless "negative reinforcement," as behaviorists term this continual saying no. A pigeon can learn more quickly than this. But before we write these people off as hopeless fools, listen to what they say as they sort the cards. They know they are botching it. A typical patient said, as he continued dealing, "Form is probably the correct solution so this [sorting by color] will be wrong, and this will be wrong, and wrong again.'' The problem is not one of imagination, or reasoning, or any of the things we normally think of as having to do with intelligence. It is an inflexibility in voluntary motor behavior that seems incredible, as though, having once decided to touch one's nose, it becomes impossible to touch one's hand instead.

Normally, people can adapt their behavior to their circumstances, as they understand them. We have seen that mental organization, or the grammar of our understanding, presides over interpretive memory. It is that grammar that orders and alters our behavior, and its proper functioning depends on the frontal cortex. When the amygdala directs a circuit into this area, it turns to the grammatical associations of interpretive memory.

In Part One we saw that interpretive memory depends on two separate types of associations. One type is the perceptual association that permits us to recognize a chunk. The other type is the grammatical association that lets us recall a chunk. For interpretive memory to function properly the brain must coordinate the actions between these two types of associations. Many of the most baffling and bizarre forms of brain damage disrupt this coordination.

The area of grammatical association is the frontal cortex. Perceptual associations continue to rest under the control of the perceptual cortex. Thus, a properly functioning interpretive memory depends on the continuing interaction of the frontal and perceptual regions of the brain. The circuit can travel from the frontal to the perceptual cortex through the thalamus, just as in the circuit for factual memory.

Now that we have seen that two brain regions support interpretive memory, perhaps we can make better sense of that peculiar test in which people with brain damage could not change their method of sorting cards. They can recognize the problem because they have suffered no damage to their perceptual cortex, but purposeful action is controlled in the brain's frontal areas. When that region is damaged, they may not be able to adapt their actions, no matter how good their perceptions are. A well-functioning interpretive memory depends on a loop that brings the separate regions of the brain into harmony.

The parts of the brain used in the basic interpretive circuit are: *perceptual cortex* (recognizes a chunk), *evaluative system* (evaluates quizzically), *amygdala* (kicks the matter upstairs), *frontal cortex* (constructs a chunk). If the circuit loops back on itself it will return to the perceptual cortex via the thalamus. It is also through this front-perception link that interpretive memories can become bothered. The grammatical associations used by the frontal cortex lead us to recall one thing, but when we construct it the perceptual cortex does not recognize what we recall. Instead of working in harmony, the two separate parts of the circuit contradict one another. We feel bothered and try to resolve the tension.

The looping through the frontal and perceptual cortex can lead to prolonged periods of concentration. Breaks in the con-centration loop can occur with a completing action (e.g., a surgeon finishes sewing a wound); an evaluation that keeps the memory on the emotional level (e.g., a writer begins to feel threatened by his own ideas and quits pursuing them); a distrac-tion that sends the circuit to the hippocampus instead of to the amygdala, turning memory to the factual level (e.g., during conversation a reference distracts the speaker and sends him on a tangent away from his point); or a "bothered" sense that grammar and recognition no longer support one another. A conscious, creative judgment may resolve this tension and per-mit resumption of the loop.

Some of the research that supports Arnold's theory was done in her own laboratory, but much was done by others in many different laboratories. Her most important contribution showed how we can organize these circuits by referring to subjective motives for the construction of a memory. Arnold is hardly alone in talking about the role of the hippocampus, amygdala, or thalamus in remembering. Her real achievement has been to show how we can unite the separate circuits into a meaningful whole if we say that subjective experiences matter. She states her own position bluntly:

> Memory is not an isolated process. It depends on perception, is influenced by emotion and imagination and embedded in the whole sequence from perception to action. Without memory, there can be no perception as we experience it, no learning, no motivated action. . . . that is the sum and substance of my theory of brain function.

It sounds almost exactly like Bartlett's remarks on imagination fifty years earlier; only Bartlett studied behavior whereas Arnold examined the brain. The study of the functioning of memory and the functioning of the brain has at last come together.

10

MEMORY STUDIES TODAY

When people disagreed with him, he urged them to be objective.

—Joseph Heller, *Catch-22*, 1961

One basic idea emerges from Alkon's work: Experience changes a neuron's activity. Arnold's work adds a second idea: The brain is organized in a way that lets us use those changes in the neuron. There is a long way to go before all the issues in this research are accepted as settled. It will take decades and many experiments before we understand human neurons as well as we do the sea snail's. We also have much to learn about the details of the brain's circuits. But it is striking to see how far already these two basic principles have penetrated into the generally accepted account of memory. The crisis that arose from the long frustrating search for the memory store is past.

In the summer of 1986 *Science,* the journal of the American Association for the Advancement of Science, published an article by Larry Squire, a San Diego psychiatrist, about memory and the brain. Squire titled his article "Mechanisms of Memory," the same title Roy John gave his pivotal book twenty years earlier. Within the first two paragraphs of the article Squire had made both points—experience changes the neuron and the brain remembers by returning its circuits to the changed neuron.

These principles are too new to be carved into stone, but they already occupy the mainstream of memory studies.

Squire continues to speak of storage. He wrote, "Memory is stored as changes in the same neural systems that ordinarily participate in perception." To my mind the reference to storage is unnecessary. All that has to be said is that experience changes the neural systems that ordinarily participate in perception, but perhaps I am quibbling about terms. The point is that already the conservative authorities agree that the old model was wrong. The word *storage* has become no more than a synonym for change, and change occurs at the site of experience. The change that supports memory does not occur in specialized storage areas that people once assumed must be part of any memory system.

Mechanical Memory

The biggest loser in this new notion of how memory works is the idea that computer memories and human memories have anything in common. The subject of mechanical "memory," the memory of computers, has long led us into bogs and briars of confusion. We snagged ourselves on a bad pun. Because every computer has a "memory," people have assumed that some of our insights into mechanical memory could help us understand biological memory. Discussions of human memory often used words drawn from computer terminology, and theorists liked to take analogies from computer operation, imagining that the metaphors could help understand the architecture of human memory; however, human and computer memories are as distinct as life and lightning.

Scientific approaches to human powers assume of course that natural laws underlie our actions. In Freud's age, naturalistic assumptions required that everything be explained in terms of matter and energy, even though many observers doubted that such basic biological processes as reproduction and metabolism could possibly depend on matter and energy alone. In the decade following the close of World War II, those doubts were justified by the discovery that reproduction and metabolism both depend on information stored in a cell's DNA. Naturalistic assumptions then urged that all human achievement be explained in terms of matter, energy, and stored information. But our survey has shown that by the time birds evolved memory had begun to replace inherited information as a guide to action. Alkon's work shows that it is not the brain but the single neuron that works like a computer, and the neuron changes its output in accordance with changes wrought by experience. We can still hope for natural explanations of human behavior, but any full account must consider matter, energy, information, and experience.

Forty years ago, when the computer first shunted onstage, the Western imagination had no vocabulary, no philosophy, and no science that could help it sort the differences between what the machines did and what people do. The bill had arrived at last for our long refusal to credit importance and prestige to our active vitality. It took decades for us to find words and a science that could distinguish between mechanical processes and living experiences.

A particularly strong source of confusion was John von Neumann's decision to refer to the computer's store of information as its "memory." Von Neumann was a great mathematician, the founder of game theory, and a key contributor to the development of the atomic bomb. During the Second World War he learned of the development of the computer and became fascinated by it. Von Neumann designed the basic computer architecture used to this day. He was the first to speak of memory in these machines, and that clumsy choice of terms has made it hard ever since for people to distinguish between what a computer's memory does (store electronic information) and what a human memory does (adapt behavior).

The two major parts of any modern computer are its central processing unit and the "memory" that stores electronic patterns. Normally people call storage space a shelf or a drawer or a warehouse, and the first computer designers did not call the information-storage machinery memory. Charles Babbage, the Victorian mathematician who first conceived of a computing machine, used the metaphor of a factory to explain his idea. He called the central unit a "mill" and the memory a "store." During the 1930s several prototype computers appeared, leading to the wartime development of a programmable computer. EN-IAC, as the working machine was known, was one of those secret World War II projects like penicillin and the atomic bomb that made the postwar world profoundly unlike prewar life. It received data via punch cards and used a series of devices called accumulators to store the working calculations. In early 1944 Presper Eckert, the Oppenheimer of the ENIAC project, described an idea he had for storing a computer program on disks: "This is similar to the tone-generating mechanism used in some electric organs and offers a permanent way of storing the basic signals required." So Eckert knew he needed storage but still did not call it memory.

When von Neumann learned of the ENIAC project, he wrote his own draft proposal for an advanced version of such a machine and he submitted his ideas in June 1945. In that draft he deliberately used the analogy of the computer as a brain. He called the parts of the computer that performed mathematical operations "specialized organs" and he compared the relays of the computer with neurons in the brain. (Von Neumann assumed that neurons were electric relays. No one then imagined that they might be capable of changing their behavior.) In this spirit of analogy von Neumann discussed the problem of programming the computer:

> Any device which is to carry out long and complicated sequences of operations (specifically of calculations) must have a considerable memory. . . . Even in the process of carrying out a multiplication or a division, a series of intermediate (partial) results must be remembered. . . . The instructions which govern a complicated problem may constitute a considerable material. . . . This material must be remembered. . . .

In this passage von Neumann's use of the words *memory* and *remembering* seem entirely casual, but then he became more direct:

> To sum up the third remark: The device requires a considerable memory. While it appears that various parts of this memory have to perform functions which differ somewhat in their nature and considerably in their purpose, it is nevertheless tempting to treat the entire memory as one organ. . . . The three specific parts C[entral] A[rithmetic part], C[entral] C[ontrol] . . . and M[emory] correspond to the *associative* neurons in the human nervous system. It remains to discuss the equivalents of the *sensory* or *afferent* and *motor* or *efferent* neurons. These are the *input* and *output* organs of the device. . . .

With this analogy, speculation about memory took a drastically wrong course. Computer memory and biological memory are profoundly different, yet because of their shared name many bright thinkers have for forty years assumed that, at bottom, the two memories must be profoundly alike. Computers have no emotional drive, no capacity to attend to experience, and no ability to recognize individual things. They operate exactly as Freud once speculated our own brains must work. Inputs pass through them without making any lasting changes. Instead of providing artificial intelligence, these machines suffer from artificial amnesia. They sit like frogs on a lily pad waiting for prescribed conditions, and they act in a prescribed manner. Memory as we know it has nothing to do with their performance.

Although no one took von Neumann's analogies literally, many students of "artificial intelligence" and cognitive psychology have viewed them as serious metaphors. Some people argued that despite the many physical differences between mechanical and animal memory, the two must share functionally similar components. This argument too can no longer stand. Human memory adapts behavior and uses emotion, attention, and insight. Computers have different functions and neither their storage systems nor their processors have any counterparts to memory's functional circuits.

Every step up memory's staircase demands some special associative power. Emotional memory requires an awareness of pleasure and pain. Factual memory begins with attention. Attention has many surprising attributes, including the way, as we learn a skill, we can turn our attention from the performance of an action to the purpose of the action. Computers have no attention to turn or purposes to turn to. If we persist in active attention, we can hope for an insight that will lift us to memory's third level. Insight discovers previously unknown associations between apparently separate chunks. It lets us take a grammar from one chunk and apply it elsewhere, creating a new chunk. Indeed, for the past generation, philosophers have argued that creative thinking means finding ways to associate ideas that had previously seemed separate.

The most famous story of such a creative discovery goes back to the ancient Greeks. The mathematician Archimedes was asked by his king to determine whether a crown was pure gold. Faced with what, by all known laws of metallurgy, seemed an impossible problem, Archimedes seemed certain to fail. Then he settled into his bath, and noticed that his presence made the bathwater rise. He suddenly saw a link between his problem and the rising bathwater: Pure gold will displace one amount of water; a gold alloy of the same size will displace a different amount. *Eureka!* he shouted and ran naked through the streets. It is an inspiring tale, one so appealing that even people who have never heard of Socrates seem to know that a Greek once ran about town shouting eureka. Thanks to Archimedes' insight we gained a new chunk of knowledge based on the principle of buoyancy.

People who venerate the computer love to pose this challenge: Imagine that you can communicate via teletype with a computer and a person. You do not know which answers come from the person and which from the machine. Can you think of a question that, in principle, a machine can never answer as well as a human? On the day you cannot find such a question, the distinction between human and machine intelligence will cease to matter.

If the teletype experiment had been done in Syracuse in about 250 B.C. we could have used Archimedes as our human and have asked, "How can the king discover whether the crown given to him is, as advertised, one of pure gold?" At the time of asking, neither the computer nor Archimedes would have had either the information or the procedures necessary to answer the question. Yet we know that Archimedes used experience and insight to find an answer, two things that, in principle, computers lack. In this experiment we see the critical difference between human memory and computer storage. Once we have acquired information and devised procedures for manipulating it, computers make wonderful tools, but we still must do the learning, adapting, and the updating. Those powers are what our memories do best, and why the search for mechanical memories to replace living ones is a dead end.

Chemical Memory

In our new understanding of memory, biochemistry has won as big a victory as computer science has lost. In his study of memory, Roy John's most firmly stated point held that "the sustained change which we call memory must be mediated by some alteration of matter, some redistribution of chemical compounds." That doctrine has triumphed. All interaction between neurons is chemical, as are all long- and short-term changes in neuron structure. When experience changes a neuron, its chemical activity changes.

The chemical changes in the neuron suggest that drugs might help a person's memory, and since most people wish their memories were more accurate, every large pharmaceutical company hopes to develop a memory pill. Memory drugs might work in a variety of ways. For example, they could help in engram formation by improving the efficiency of damaged neurons, or by restoring a neuron's weakened capacity to emit a particular chemical, or by maintaining a neuron's ability to change in response to experiences. Any of these strategies may prove effective. Rumors in the pharmaceutical industry suggest that a memory drug for some victims of stroke may become available before the decade of the 1980s is out.

Yet we must remember that memory is not one single thing. Its many levels depend on one another, but they are distinct. During the Renaissance, too, physicians and alchemists hoped to find a potion that would help a person remember better. Rosemary and a variety of other herbs were said to have the power of memory. Today, however, the idea of a pill that simply permits a person to "remember better" sounds as naive as the hope that hypnosis can make a person remember better. We cannot seriously hope to find a drug that will guarantee the correct reconstruction of an experience.

It is easier to disrupt emotional memory than to establish a desire artificially, so the first emotional-memory drug is more likely to induce amnesia than to improve memory. This use may seem strange, but survival sometimes depends on an ability to endure the awful without panic. A particularly notable example comes from childbirth. If the pain of delivery stayed fresh in memory, each new labor in a woman's life might be greeted with increasingly uncontrollable terror; however, during labor the uterus releases massive amounts of a hormone, oxytocin, and apparently this natural drug induces extensive forgetting of the childbirth experience. Although each of us knows exceptions to this rule, the gospel parable about women forgetting the pain of childbirth seems literally true in many cases. Drugs that block formation of terrible associations may gain a place in treating victims of particularly brutal shocks.

Drugs that work in the opposite direction—promoting emotional associations—are more difficult to identify. Many people do form emotional attachments to drugs themselves, but a drug that leads to an emotional association with some other person or experience seems more difficult to sustain. Such a discovery would constitute a love potion and is not near to hand.

Factual memory would improve if we paid more attention to things, so drugs that increase arousal might improve memory automatically. Caffeine is well known as a stimulant, and research has established that taking caffeine enhances memory in the laboratory. One current research project studies a caffeine medication 100,000 times more arousing than a cup of coffee, without the side effects on blood pressure. Another common drug that seems to improve attention and memory is nicotine. Smoking a cigarette just before presentation of a fifty-word list improves recall after intervals of ten and forty-five minutes. Higher nicotine cigarettes are more effective than low nicotine brands. There are many good reasons for not smoking, but under laboratory conditions, nicotine can improve one's factual recall.

Another approach to improving factual memory might try to speed up the rate at which we associate experiences. We know that somehow the hippocampus consolidates associations so that one experience reminds us of another, and it might be possible to increase the rate at which the hippocampus does its work. One hormone that may speed up the formation of factual associations is arginine vasopressin, a hormone secreted by the pituitary. Another chemical, one related to vasopressin, also helps factual memory, but only in males. Why a particular chemical should affect one sex and not another remains a mystery. It often happens too that the effectiveness of a drug depends on a precise dosage. Too much or too little has no result. The complexity of the brain suggests that although the first memory drugs may appear at any moment, new drugs will continue to appear for many years. By this century's end, memory drugs are likely to be familiar, but two decades into the next century, all twentieth-century memory drugs may seem primitive.

There is, however, something tragically naive in the hope of using drugs to artificially improve factual memory. Drugs may stimulate us, but attention still requires an initial curiosity, and as we pay attention, we must continue to feel curious and interested. Arousal by itself does not guarantee attention to what we are supposed to attend. The college student of the future who takes a memory pill before listening to a lecture may find that he is alert to everything but the boring lecture. The secret of attention, the quality that distinguishes it from the input device on a computer, is its selectivity. We base our selections on emotional memory. We can bring some discipline to the activity, but surprisingly little. Selective attention permits us to concentrate on the things that matter to us and ignore the things that do not. Almost certainly, drugs will one day help people whose damaged brain functions impair their memories, but drugs may never do much more than that. The whole point of memory's evolution has been to pull us beyond our own internal assumptions so we can see and use what stands out there in the world beyond our skin. Drugs produce their effects without reference to what occurs beyond that skin, making them profoundly anti-memory.

Active Memory

At present the biggest dispute in memory studies concerns the active role of memory's separate functions. Roy John doubted that functions were localized, but that argument is over. Today, few investigators seriously question the idea that there are different kinds of memory dependent on different areas of the brain. Researchers also agree that some kinds of memory have a much older evolutionary history than others and that some kinds develop sooner in children than others. There is even agreement that different areas produce different subjective experiences. Squire's survey of memory, for example, said, "This notion [of different kinds of memory] necessarily accepts the concepts of conscious and unconscious memory as serious topics for experimental work." But there is considerable disagreement over whether these subjective experiences matter to the construction of a memory.

In this book I have followed Arnold's principles for organizing memories. They lead to the staircase of dependent levels we saw in Part One, but Arnold has a very active view of memory. Desire, attention, and judgment all play important roles in her theory. Many memory theorists deny that subjective processes can help us understand either the workings of memory or the relation between the different kinds of memory.

The dispute comes down to the passive or active question. If memory is entirely passive, manipulated only by objective factors, the brain is a machine. It is not a computer or a tape recorder, but it is a biochemical device and its activity comes from outside itself. Many people insist that it is unscientific to deny that the brain is a machine. The repeated use of the title "Mechanisms of Memory" is an aggressive assertion that memory is part of the dead mechanical universe. These thinkers will not lightly embrace a view of an active memory whose adaptations depend on subjective factors known only to the individual actor.

Every step up the memory staircase, however, depends on a subjective factor—awareness of pleasure and pain, emotion, recalled perception, insight, and judgment. Arnold was extremely bold to include such factors in her circuits. They change behavior from mechanical output to a creative performance. In this active view the brain is like a piano and memory is like the replaying of a tune. Instead of retrieving images, memory gives us a performance. Instead of preserving old images, memory gives us new ways to perform. This metaphor would once have seemed impossible for it immediately raises the question of who plays the piano. Do we have a little man in our head? Today, however, we know enough to see that the neurons perform in their millions and billions along the memory circuits.

Is memory a machine or a performance? In time, I believe, memory scholars generally will resolve this dispute in favor of performance, of an active memory. I am no prophet, but events seem to flow toward common acceptance of Frederick Bartlett's position that subjective factors are as important as objective ones. Even a conservative like Larry Squire finds himself forced by the evidence to acknowledge a subjective presence, and if it is present why have we evolved it? Is it an ornament, an appendix that has always been irrelevant to survival? The suggestion seems unlikely on its face, and Arnold's theory depicts an evolutionary advantage that comes from these subjective factors. They provide new powers for adapting to the environment. The active view of memory enables us to make sense of its evolution among species and its development in the individual. In Part Three we shall also see that it helps to make sense of forgetting, traditionally one of memory's most puzzling problems. But for all its strengths, the active view changes our understanding of scientific explanation.

Subjective factors have crept into one area of psychology after another. Even emotion was once a taboo subject for mainstream psychology, but that day has passed. By the mid 1970s the subject had become so respectable it got its own scholarly journal, *Motivation and Emotion*. Meanwhile, other psychologists have reconsidered the matter of attention. Theories that seek an objective explanation for attention see it as a process of filtering input. Computers can do that much, responding only to digits, for example. But increasing numbers of scholars have concluded that attention is a subjective selection of what to take in. This group says, for example, that at a cocktail party people actively select the sounds made by the person they are speaking with. We choose what we listen to. The most respected figure in this reconsideration of attention has been Ulric Neisser, one of the leaders in the development of cognitive psychology. In 1976 he published a book expressing his disappointment over the way cognitive psychology had developed. In criticizing theories that said attention was objectively programmed into the brain, Neisser complained:

The villains of the piece are the mechanistic information-processing models, which treat the mind as a fixed-capacity device for converting discreet and meaningless inputs into conscious percepts.

And Neisser closed his chapter about attention with the words, "Consciousness is an aspect of mental activity, not a switching center on the intrapsychic railway." Bartlett could not have said it more insistently.

Insight, creativity, and the perception of symbols have always posed challenges for thinkers who insist that only objective stimuli control thought. B. F. Skinner boldly denied that creativity exists, but few other psychologists have gone that far. Most of those who concentrate on the objective side of behavior have preferred to ignore creativity, a problem to consider later. Subjectivity was never seriously exorcised from this field, and we saw in Part One that the first principle of interpretive memory holds that subjective organization presides over this level of memory.

Memory study has reached a crossroad similar to the one physics reached sixty years ago. Until the 1920s all physics, all science, assumed that everything in the universe was determined by strict cause-and-effect relations. Then quantum mechanics appeared and replaced determinism with uncertainty. The idea so scandalized Einstein that he spent the rest of his life vainly trying to refute it, but other physicists saw the practical value of the idea and used it. Today physics without uncertainty is unthinkable. A similar challenge faces memory study. Until recently all science has assumed that only objective factors control events. Now we find that we can explain much about memory if we add subjectivity to the account. Some people, perhaps some of psychology's deepest thinkers, will never accept the idea. Many people have devoted their professional lives to projects of artificial intelligence and to the metaphors of cognitive psychology. Some of them will surely resist suggestions that imagination holds the secret of memory. Today we can only wait to see if they will find a refutation to subjectivity's importance.

PART THREE

THE FORGETTERY

11

ORDINARY
"FORGETTING"

I know very well that people won't forget. It's natural to
think that they might, since they forget most everything
else. . . . From what I've seen, usually people only
remember something if they was around personally at the
time; or maybe if their father was around. . . . But nobody
ever forgets the "Black Sox," and that's the truth.

—Harry Stein, *Hoopla,* 1983

Most discussions of the memory problems in every-
day life begin with an exaggerated faith in ordinary remembering
and understanding. If you assume, for example, that it is easy
to remember your intentions, then a forgotten intention becomes
a puzzle. Yet everyone has found himself standing in a familiar
room wondering what on earth he came to fetch. We forget
contexts and we forget actions. Our continual forgetting of
things little and large is a great annoyance. Then we double the
burden by imagining that the difficulties are peculiar.

True memory breakdowns are so bizarre that almost anybody can spot them. They show themselves as an inability to
move up through the levels of memory. For example, a person
may be unable to form new factual associations. A patient with
amnesia must be reintroduced to his doctor each time they meet,
even if they have been meeting for years. It is needlessly cruel
to tell an amnesiac about a death in the family. He may be

moved to tears and feel a deep sense of loss, but he will forget, and the next time someone mentions the death the news will be just as shocking as the first time. Even after the twentieth time, the news comes as an unexpected, unsoftened blow.

Ordinary forgetting is nothing like this. We may forget the name of everyone we met at last night's party, but we remember that there was a party. We can forget being told to do something, and may not even recognize the instruction when it is repeated later. But we can remember something that did hold our attention—the magazine we were reading, for example—back when we ignored the instruction. Ordinary forgetting is the routine failure to use the memory powers that we have. Pathological forgetting is the loss of one of memory's powers. The difference is as palpable as the difference between not using your fingers and having no fingers.

We have seen that remembering is a much more active process than the old storage metaphor supposed. To construct our memories we need arousal and understanding. Forgetting, by contrast, is more passive than we realized. A popular joke on Washington's Capitol Hill holds that although a politician needs a good memory, he needs an even better "forgettery" that actively denies the many sins of his past. But usually forgetting is not so creative. Just as cold is the absence of heat, so forgetting is the absence of remembering.

When it seemed as though remembering was just a matter of retrieval from storage, philosophers asked what happened to disrupt retrieval. Did we drop the item? (Indeed, in its Germanic origins *forget* means to lose hold of.) Many researchers have tried to find active explanations for forgetting. Perhaps we retrieve the wrong thing or misplace an item in storage or unconsciously refuse to retrieve it. Perhaps items in storage fade with time or perhaps over time associations break apart. Each of these ideas has had its defenders, but looking for a cause of forgetting is like looking for the cause of darkness on a moonless night. Instead of asking what happened to cause the darkness, we must wonder why there is no moon. Instead of asking what happened to cause forgetting, we must look for what would have caused remembering had it not been absent.

It is in the consideration of forgetting that we see immediately how the world of memory studies has been turned upside down. Many of the pillars of the revolution hardly seem radical. Common sense tells us that emotions, perceptions, and reminders are all important to memory, but the old theories ignored these points and developed as though they did not exist.

Emotions, perceptions, and reminders all stir the imagination, and imagination, not storage, is the basis of memory. If we try to remember a name and cannot, we search for reminders that will help. We try to construct as many details as we can in the hope that they will help us remember. Many students discover that if the teacher asks a question and they have forgotten the answer, they may remember just by starting to reply. Construction of the answer produces it. Forgetting is the absence of that construction.

Contrast this forgetting with that of a computer that does use storage. I have a computer myself and once even wrote a short program that retrieves data that had seemed hopelessly lost. A danger of word processors is that something can go wrong and all one's work evaporates into some electronic limbo. Former president Jimmy Carter lost drafts of several early chapters to his memoirs that way. Believe me, it is maddening to see all your prose disappear in the twinkling of an electronic glitch. On my word processor, however, there is a secret storage area where the text survives, so I wrote a little program for emergencies. It gets into that secret area and retrieves the lost text. The first time I saw the vaporized text come rolling across my computer screen I felt like a man who had summoned the dead from their tombs, but it was no miracle. When difficulties arise with stored information, the problem is always to find out where the stored data lies. Problems with remembering, however, require a different approach. We need to assist our imagination.

Missing Reminders

Memory begins when some aspect of present experience triggers an association. At the level of emotional memory an experience may evoke an emotion, at the factual and interpretive levels it may evoke an image or a symbol, respectively. Whatever the level, memory begins with reminders. We saw that artificial memory starts by inventing reminders. Artificial forgetting begins by removing them. If we want to help people forget something, we first try to remove likely reminders from their surroundings. It is said that Las Vegas casinos have no clocks and that croupiers wear no watches, in order not to remind gamblers of the time. At the other extreme, airports and depots are full of clocks to help travelers remember that time passes and that it matters.

Suppose we want something and go to the bedroom to fetch it. We arrive. Now what did we come to get? I have asked myself that question too many times. We need a reminder to remember what we came for, but we left the original reminder back in the room we just came from. If we go back to that room, it will probably remind us again, but going back means extra work and leaves us feeling foolish. If the item we seek lies in plain view, it can serve as its own reminder. But if we do not notice it we have no reminder. A potential third reminder is some mental association. When we arrive in the room, the room itself reminds us, "I came for X," but mental associations form only if we paid attention at the outset. If we do not attend to the point of the task when we head off to the room, the room will not remind us of what we came to get.

Without reminders, memory is doomed. Even if we have paid close attention to something, we need a reminder to trigger its memory. Freud said that the best proof that memory needs more than attention comes from the forgetting of intentions. We may plan something, may even discuss it, and yet we forget it. He cited the example of a lover who fails to keep a rendezvous, and he warned that the lover should not say, "I forgot," in defense. The other will reply, "A year ago you would not have forgotten." Touché! A year ago everything seemed to trigger thoughts of one's lover, but today that passion has cooled. Freud himself believed that all memories are stored and that retrieval is automatic unless blocked. The forgotten rendezvous, he said, shows a deliberate (although perhaps unconscious) intent to forget. Our new understanding of memory softens that harsh judgment. Love's obsession has cooled, but that need not imply active scorn. We need reminders to remember even the things we want most.

Missing Attention

Reminders trigger associations and associations begin with attention. In Chapter 4 we saw that William James defined attention as "the taking possession" of parts of an experience. His active metaphor agrees with our own view of memory as doing. Attention is like digestion. We do not store the food we eat; we break it down so that it becomes part of our body. Attention selects parts of experience and uses it to nourish our memories. We do not store this experience, we use it. Of course, we eat many things that we do not digest and we also experience many things without paying them any attention.

We get into quick trouble if we imagine inattention as a refusal to eat, as a kind of sensory filter that keeps some things from entering our brains. Psychologists have searched closely for such filters and never found them. Attention actively takes in. It does not just keep perceptions out. Every mother knows the problems that arise from the naive view that perception implies attention. A mother can tell a child, "I want you to do so-and-so." The child listens and forgets. It is not that the child did not hear the instructions. He did. He did not, however, actively seize them and make them his. Attention is an aroused response to experience, and most things do not arouse us. Or, if they do, they do not arouse us for long.

The most common distraction is probably concern for oneself. When two people meet, their attention tends to focus on themselves. Outwardly they seem alert. They smile, shake hands, look each other in the eye, and say their names aloud. Inwardly, a person may even think he is paying attention to the other because he sees and hears that other person. But the display of interest is automatic. Meanwhile the other person also pays attention to himself, to looking good and making a good impression. When both people seek to make a fine impression, neither makes any and both forget the exchange in an instant.

Actors and actresses at auditions often show this type of self-concerned distraction in a memory failure known as the next-in-line effect. After trying out for a part, performers may remember many other people's auditions but they find it nearly impossible to remember the tryout just before their own. Normally people at an audition worry about their own performance. As they have little else to do and they feel curious about the competition, they generally watch the other performers, but when their own turn comes nearly due, they concentrate on getting ready. The next in line serves primarily as a cue, indicating the time for them to start. If a person had to, he could pay attention to the next in line and remember what the person said or did. But people normally have no special reason to pay attention.

Experiments have shown that the next-in-line effect also occurs during laboratory procedures. In one such experiment, researchers assembled groups of people to read lists of words. In some groups, participants knew the order of their performance. In other groups, participants did not know when they would be called on to read. Only people who knew their order of performance showed a marked next-in-line effect, and experimenters abolished the effect by the simple expedient of telling people they would be questioned about the list read just ahead of them, in effect, giving them a reason to pay attention.

Similar self-distractions probably lie behind the stereotypi-
cal problems of the "absentminded professor." In these situations a person quickly forgets information or instructions even
though he seemed to be paying attention when he originally
received the information. Paying attention requires more than
listening. When a person's thoughts are interrupted, he must go
through a two-step process. First, he must put his old thoughts
on hold; second, he must actively digest the new information. It
is not enough to put thoughts on hold and hear the new information. Attention means listening—perceiving, judging, thinking
about.

In a setting where interruptions have become common,
attention requires deliberate effort. People who need to practice
paying attention should begin by exaggerating their involvement.
"I'm going to listen," says the interrupted person, and he
attends carefully, putting other thoughts aside for the duration
of the interruption and considering precisely what he hears and
imagining himself performing the instruction. Paying attention is
work. We do ourselves an injustice by assuming that passive
listening is enough.

Even when we pay enough attention to learn something we
never learn the whole context of an experience. There are
always flies buzzing in the corner or cracks on the ceiling that
we ignore. Often we form only the barest associations. This
partial learning has a built-in benefit, for partial knowledge is
generalized knowledge. It carries few associations and travels
from context to context without difficulty. This transfer matters
particularly in the use of symbols like words. Adults know many
thousands of words, but can tell how they came to know only a
few of them. Of English words, I believe I can recall the origins
of my knowledge for precisely one—*punctual*. Unfortunately,
my memory on the point is so clear that I have problems using
the word. Whenever I hear it, I remember when I was seven
years old excitedly waiting to see my first major league baseball
game. My parents and I waited for a fourth person (known to
my memory only as "the Yugoslav"), who was late. My father
said, "He is usually so punctual," and I asked what that word

meant. Believe me, it is a nuisance to have so powerful an association that the mere sound of a word transports me back to the gate at Griffith Stadium (a gate torn down decades ago). Words have to be used in a more generalized way. Languages would hardly work if every word provoked such specific memories of past acquaintance. Interpretive memory depends on our ability to combine symbols whose origins we do not recall according to a grammar we cannot explain.

Experiments have long demonstrated our tendency to ignore sources of information. Researchers originally called this poor memory "interference," reflecting the old assumption that a memory problem indicates some difficulty in retrieval. Psychologists first observed memory's generalizing tendency in studies that presented subjects with several lists to learn. Subjects confuse the lists, mixing early lists with later ones and later lists with earlier ones.

We tend to remember similar experiences as a piece and cannot easily distinguish one from the other unless we have paid attention to some quality that makes it unique. Although this tendency confuses any precise memory for particular past events, it enriches our general appreciation for the possibilities of experience. We learn and associate details with a generalized version of an experience and become ready for a broader range of possibilities the next time something similar occurs. Thanks to partial learning we can acquire a skill and need not be too particular about the setting in which we practice it.

In the early days of learning a skill we must pay close attention to our actions. When we first learn to type, for example, we search out every key and then calculate which finger we should use. We pay close attention to the keyboard then. The same holds true when learning to drive with a stick shift. We have to pay close attention to coordinating our foot movement with the proper hand action, but in time we learn these actions so well that we need not pay them any attention. The skilled typist and experienced driver treat their machines as though they ran automatically, obeying their wish like the humblest servant. Like some god-king of old, the typist says, "I merely have to think 'C-a-l-l- -m-e- -I-s-h-m-a-e-l' and it is typed.'' Of course, the body still controls and directs all this activity, but the events are too quick and precise for conscious direction or even for feedback control. We act without attention. The discovery that action does not imply attention was an important turning point in modern psychology. In 1948, Karl Lashley argued that instead of making us attentive, automatically organized behavior disengages us from the world. Psychologists buzzed in consternation. At that time the dominant school of thought held that the environment controls every detail of an action. Today, the concern runs in the other direction as we see just how much of our behavior is automatic. Does learning turn us into robots?

Many memory failures reflect exactly this danger. Absent-mindedness generally indicates inattentive mechanical behavior. Typically, its problems arise amid familiar surroundings, when doing something well practiced. Situations like these dampen attention. The familiar setting and routine behavior keep the orientation reaction at bay. And if anything else catches our attention, we may ignore entirely the automatic action of putting aside our keys or wallet. Only later do we wonder where we put these things.

If we set out to do something and then let our attention wander, some automatic action may intrude on our behavior. We may head off to a hardware store and find ourselves standing in the grocery store instead. The habit of going to the grocery store has intruded on the plan. Our mind attended to something other than making sure that we went to the right place. Habit has taken over, and suddenly we have arrived in the grocery store.

To prevent a skill from becoming robotic we must continue to pay attention to our actions. Typists who know the keyboard no longer have to think about finding a letter or which finger to use, but must continue to give attention to their copy. An experienced driver no longer thinks about how to coordinate foot and hand maneuvers, but continues to pay attention to the traffic.

Actions based on interpretive memory absolutely depend on an ability to act and continue paying attention. Insights carry us to memory's top level; concentration keeps us there. Lower levels have essentially one attention-action cycle:

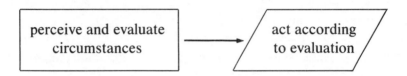

But on the interpretive level we imagine our intention and can redirect our attention to suit the changing situation.

A classic case that shows the need for interpretive attention comes from a woman who worked for years filleting fish and then suffered frontal lobe damage that disrupted her interpretive memory. The fish continued to remind her of her job and she would pick up a fish as though to fillet it, but then could not continue. She might make a stab or two, but the purposeful act of filleting a fish was beyond her. After picking up the fish she would put it down and pick up another. The reminder got her started, but she could not imagine the purpose she was after and could not finish her work. She found similar problems at home. She would start her domestic chores but could not complete them. She would pick up a sugar bowl as though to put it away and then not know what to do with it. Sometimes she set it down in the refrigerator.

Some animals too can adjust their attention to a small degree. The most dramatic shifts occur among hunting animals. They can persist in a hunt, while changing tactics. One pair of wildlife photographers observed a young male lion as it developed this flexibility. The lion had left the pride and had to feed himself. It took him several weeks to make his first kill, and he was in danger of starving. He began his hunting efforts by charging vainly at a crowded water hole. At first he simply charged and then gave up when his original prey got away. He succeeded at last when he did not stop after his initial failure, but switched his attention in mid-charge and noticed a small zebra that could not escape. This continued evaluation permits a creature to adapt its behavior even after it has started to act. The non-primate portion of the animal world seldom gets more flexible than this. In this situation, action does not put an end to purpose. The attention-action cycle repeats itself:

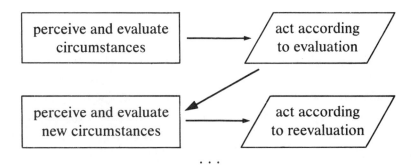

Our primate ancestors were probably never as lethal as a lion, but life in the trees demands concentration. Any creature who starts leaping from branch to branch must either concentrate or risk falling to the ground.

People can maintain these attention-action cycles for hours at a time. Philosophers often think of concentration as purely an intellectual activity, but skilled athletes do it too. Pitcher Jim Kaat, whose major-league career lasted twenty-five years, says, "Control [of the ball] is a matter of concentration." It sounds like the gibberish athletes often spout, until you understand it as referring to the attention-action cycle. As the pitcher begins to throw, he continues to pay attention to the situation and continues to evaluate what he sees.

Because concentration is a period of prolonged attention, we might suppose that we have super-memories for such experiences. Instead we are almost amnesic for them. I know this paradox from long experience as a professional writer. I devote hours every day to writing, yet if anybody asks me for the details of what I have done, I can hardly remember. Even when I see the manuscript I do not recall many of the moments of actual writing. When I write, I concentrate on expression and pay no attention to my hand as it flies along, setting my expression before me. Neither do I attend to its motions when I mark up a page. Those details are irrelevant to my purposes, and when I see a heavily reworked page I often feel surprised by the number of changes I made.

Professional athletes call this experience of super-focused attention "the tunnel." Football players talk about running through a tunnel in which they perceive only their immediate situation and what to do about it. Perhaps the clearest look the sport fan gets of the fact of this intense concentration is at a baseball game when three fielders collide while trying to catch a pop fly. Everybody in the stands can see that the men are rushing toward one another, but none of the three sees it, hears it, or feels it. Each has brought only the ball into his awareness.

Laboratory studies of concentration find the same thing. Psychologists study concentration with a technique called shadowing. Subjects listen to a message through earphones and repeat the message aloud as they listen. Experimenters can introduce different problems to make the task more challenging. A shadow word can start at the left ear and finish at the right. The message can come with a distractor. One voice says into the right ear, "In summary, although frontal lobe lesions . . . ," and the subject repeats that aloud while another voice whispers simultaneously into the left ear, "Halfway down the Rue Vercingetorix a tall guy . . . ," and the subject ignores those words. We can change the task, whispering the to-be-shadowed message into one ear while shouting the distractor message into the other. We can change the task again, requiring the subject to recite one message as usual and write down the other. Yes, amazingly enough, it is possible to learn to repeat one thing aloud while writing something else down at the same time. During the days of the moon exploration it was widely reported (and widely doubted) that newscaster Walter Cronkite could speak into the camera while receiving information from two different sources whispering via earpieces into his ears. Research shows that subjects can do all this work, and more. What they cannot do is remember what they heard and repeated. If we ask a subject what the shadowed messages said, he does not know. I have seen the same thing among typists. The better their skills, the less typists remember of what they typed. Concentration of this sort ignores most details of an experience to focus exclusively on how to accomplish one's aims.

The critical aspect of all these tasks is that they are purposeful. The lion on the hunt, the orangutan in the tree, the pitcher on the mound, the writer marking up a page, and the experimental subject shadowing a message all have to act and keep on acting. They need to develop skills, and they do. A person who simultaneously recites the words coming into his right ear and writes the words heard in the left is a skilled wonder. When laboratory experiments first tackled the task, neither the subjects nor the experimenters believed it was possible. But the subjects learned how to do it. The meaning of whatever they repeated was irrelevant to their purposes, however; shadowing is quite unlike going to a theater and watching a movie for two hours. In that setting, meaning is all and many people upon leaving a theater can recite much of the film's plot. Of course they went there to learn a good story. On the other hand, even regular movie fans might find it quite difficult to watch a movie and repeat every word spoken immediately after hearing it. Shadowing words is a skill that takes intense concentration. The experimental subject ignores everything that seems irrelevant to the task, including the meaning of the shadowed message. It should hardly surprise us to discover that after ignoring meaning, subjects do not remember it.

Normal Memories

Naturally, people who suffer from frequent bouts of absent-mindedness wish they had more satisfactory memories. Conventional wisdom urges people not to make too much of ordinary forgetting. We know from close studies of everyday memory that absentmindedness is a regular part of normal life. If we realized how often absentmindedness affected other people, we would appreciate that our own slips are nothing special. But this advice is easier to give than to receive. We want to control events, or at least control ourselves. When memory works right, it gives us that control. When it does not work right, we cannot expect to be cheered by the thought that control is hard for everybody.

The advice about not worrying may even contribute to the problem. It says pay no attention to your problem, and your problem is that you do not pay enough attention to your actions. Memory students should not act like the Great Oz shouting authoritatively, "Pay no attention to that little man behind the curtain." People should pay attention, but in a fruitful way.

Ordinary forgetting does not imply stupidity, creeping senility, or even not caring. You have not forgotten where you put your keys because unconsciously you do not really want to find them. You forget because you did not notice where you put them. So practice noticing. Take your keys from your pocket and notice where you set them down.

I am sometimes absentminded myself and well know the sense of impotent despair that comes from looking for a piece of paper that I held in my hand not ten seconds ago. Only when I began working on this book, however, did it cross my mind that absentmindedness need not be a fate assigned by the gods. If it came from unnoticed automatic actions, perhaps I could practice noticing my actions. As I put something down, I would notice, "I'm putting this here," and, by Jove, it works. I find things more readily now. I still make absentminded errors on occasion, but the occasions are fewer.

I did the same thing with the problem of habit intrusion. The place where I found the problem most annoying was at a particular subway station where I often change trains. Usually, I transfer downtown, but sometimes I switch to an uptown train. Usually I take one particular train, but sometimes I use another line that arrives on the same platform. I have discovered from painful experience that I can automatically walk to the downtown platform when I want to go uptown, or let a train go by that I wanted to take. For years, I just accepted this plight as one of my mental defects, but stirred by my own investigations, I decided to try to overcome the problem by deliberate attention. As my original train arrived at the station I began consciously reminding myself of my travel plans. At first I used complete sentences about where I was going and how to get there; now a quick shorthand does the trick. At first I had to remember to remind myself. Now the simple act of arriving in the station serves to remind me that I should remind myself of my destination and route.

A few years ago it would have embarrassed me—even in the privacy of my own brain—to think that I had to act so deliberately. I would have felt like some fool in a Charles Dickens story who wanders all the way across London reciting aloud a five-word sentence so he can give the message to someone who needs it. But remembering is hard work. We cannot take it for granted. Now I feel more like a shortstop who is in every play because, each time the pitcher begins to throw, he orients himself. To remember more, digest more and then fill the world with reminders.

12

FORGOTTEN CHUNKS:

THE FAILURE OF INTERPRETIVE MEMORY

> . . . she couldn't think of a single reason why they hadn't
> thought of looking there. This vacuum was disturbing. It
> was like reaching out for someone and finding that your
> hand had been cut off at the wrist.
>
> —Thomas Williams, *The Moon Pinnace*, 1986

Reminders and attention work only when a person can move up and down the levels of memory. If something prevents such travel, catastrophic memory failures begin to show themselves. These failures tell us most clearly what each level accomplishes. In this chapter and the following two we will examine the problems that come when people lose the ability to use part of memory. Each step on the staircase depends on those below it, so damage to a low step affects performance on the higher ones too. Thus, pathological forgetting often shows a confusing host of symptoms. Some memory may survive, but other seemingly unrelated types of remembering are lost. The farther down the memory levels we go, the more general the problems become. A person with damaged memory at the interpretive level may have an amazingly specific problem, such as the inability to remember names of fruits. Someone with factual level damage may suffer from so general a disability that, along with not remembering the names of fruits, he cannot recall what he did five minutes earlier or recognize his mother or even respond to his own name. Because forgetting on any level implies problems on higher levels too, we will start at the top of the staircase with interpretive memory where the problems are most specific.

Interpretive memory begins with an insight that unifies recall and recognition. Without that level, chunked memory is forgotten. Chunks permit purposeful behavior, so when they fail so does purposeful action. A chunk of spatial memory, for example, permits a person to follow routes he has never previously taken. He can remember his destination and understand how to move toward it. Without interpretive memory, the same person could still move about, still find his way to many places, but such movement would depend on factual memory for past experience. It would follow only practiced paths, and there would be many places "you can't get to from here."

Damage to memory's interpretive level always implies an inability to construct a chunk. With so many possible chunks, people seldom lose the ability to create any at all, but partial forgetting is common. Indeed it must be unusual for a person to discover how to create all possible chunks. Many normal people, for example, cannot achieve any musical insights. They can enjoy music's rhythms and harmonies, even "hear" tunes playing in their head, but cannot imagine new melodies, new harmonies, or new ways to perform music. If this lack of insight comes from inborn limitations, nobody is likely to notice, but if the problem comes from an injury, we can see the remnants of shattered insights. For example, Maurice Ravel, the composer of "Bolero," was in a terrible automobile accident. He survived for most of another decade but never again composed music, yet he continued to enjoy listening to music. In his case, his constructive power had gone, yet he continued to apprehend chunks. The reverse problem—an inability to recognize chunks, but a capacity to produce them—seems even stranger and perhaps more terrifying. Such a person might, for example, fail to recognize even a single passage from the Bible, but be able to recite long biblical passages.

Normal memories treat the grammatical and perceptual associations of a chunk as so much of a piece that we seldom think about the insights needed to understand them, yet using something even as ordinary as a jar depends on interpretive memory. A jar's simple grammar is the relation between the storage bowl and the lid. When we see a sealed jar, we remember its use and can imagine the same jar with the lid unscrewed.

Suppose a cabin-raiding bear finds a jar of honey. Factual memory may be enough to set the bear to work. It sees the jar and remembers honey found in similar jars, so it smashes the jar to the floor as it has done in the past. Presumably, people too could use only factual memory to open jars. A person sees the jar; the jar reminds him of the contents; he wants the contents and makes the necessary gripping and twisting motions to unscrew the lid and reveal the contents. But with interpretive memory we act from understanding as well as desire. Emotions tell us that we want the contents of the jar. Understanding tells us that we want to remove the lid from the jar. This second memory helps us if we meet trouble opening the jar. If the usual actions fail us, instead of smashing the jar, we seek other ways of removing the lid.

In this example we see the basic difference between objective reminders and subjective purposes. A reminder triggers a factual memory and results in an action. A purpose is the subjective construction of interpretive memory. A person acting on the interpretive level depends on a private purpose, not a visible reminder, to guide his progress. Wrestling with a jar shows interpretive memory at its most ordinary, but some brain-damaged people cannot remember the chunk that lets them open a jar. People with ideokinetic apraxia can perform an action like unscrewing a jar, but they cannot simply pretend to do the action with an imaginary jar. The apraxia has destroyed their memory for the purpose behind an unscrewing action. Since factual memory survives, the physical presence of the jar serves as a trigger to remind them of how to act and they can still open a jar. But pretend actions require a memory for the purpose that lies behind the action. Without interpretive memory they forget the purpose of things, so creative and playful actions disappear.

Neither science nor philosophy has analyzed most of the chunks that fill our daily lives. The most prominent exception has come from linguists who have analyzed many aspects of how language works. Even though their field developed along a line wholly unrelated to memory studies, linguistic analysis of language agrees with our findings about interpretive memory. The basic unit of linguistic analysis is the sentence. Like other chunks, sentences can combine to form still larger chunks of paragraphs and essays. The sentence fuses two separate components—grammar and meaning—into one whole. Thanks to the detailed study of language, the best descriptions of problems with damaged interpretive memories concern language problems.

Sometimes a person's power of grammatical association fails. In those cases, the person can recognize grammatical speech but cannot speak grammatically. He cannot recall the words he needs to use. Other times, perceptual association fails and a person can produce grammatically correct sentences, but cannot understand them. This last problem is particularly surprising because we have usually assumed that understanding controls grammar. But grammar and understanding are equal parts of a linguistic chunk. Each supports the other.

Lost Grammar

Memory chunks work like zippers. They consist of two separate strands bound together as a unit. These are magic zippers whose connecting teeth appear only as we imagine them and disappear as we imagine the succeeding teeth. But apart from their insubstantial side, chunk-zippers work and fail much like ordinary ones. Sometimes a zipper acquires a snag and, although it continues to function, the zipper always leaves a hole at one particular spot. Chunks can fail in the same way, damaging the recall-recognition interaction. Perceptual and grammatical associations no longer combine at that point, leaving a memory hole. In optical aphasia visual perception no longer reminds a person of a name. We know that recognition survives because we can see the person react in other ways. A person seeing a bowl of ice cream might lick his lips and smile, but cannot name what he sees. We also know that recall survives because other reminders still work. If the person touches, tastes, or smells the ice cream, he can name it. Yet the interaction between visual recognition and verbal recall has gone.

More severe cases destroy one side of the zipper. Sometimes the ability to recognize perceptual associations goes. Other times, recall's power of grammatical association fails. One study examined a patient referred to as R. H. While serving in Vietnam he had been shot in the head and thereafter he could no longer speak either fluently or grammatically. Typical of his speech was this account of his mother's death six months after his fifteenth birthday.

> My uh mother died uh me uh fifteen uh oh I guess six month my mother pass away. An uh anen uh oh uh seventeen seventeen ro uh high school an uh Christmas well uh I uh Pittburg an uh an uh anen I hitchhike uh ba uh (long pause) uh Baltimore an stay all night an'en I lef for Florida

Speech like this is painful even to read, in part because it so obviously troubles the speaker. Grammar seems forgotten, but R. H. sees its absence and tries, pretty much in vain, to correct himself. The capacity to use grammatical associations has gone. R. H. could follow and understand conversations, but he could hardly read a sentence and, when asked to listen to long stories, he could not understand them when sentences turned into paragraphs.

His problem in understanding long speech matches his inability to construct grammatical sentences. He could recognize the meaning of a single sentence, but listening is a creative process. The perceptual side of R. H.'s zipper-chunk seemed to be normal, and he could recognize words or phrases. When he heard another phrase, he could recognize it too. But without grammar he could no longer imagine how to get from the first recognition to the second. Comprehension, of course, broke down. Ordinarily we can remember what a person said because we understood him and we understood him because we constructed a chunk as we listened.

We can find similar problems in epilepsy patients whose brains have been surgically severed so that the two halves no longer communicate. Apparently the left half of the brain handles the grammatical associations that construct a chunk. (At least this principle holds true for severe epileptics, but their brains may not be organized in a normal way.) If we show a split-brain patient a ball in such a way that only the right half of the brain perceives it, the patient cannot name what he sees. But if we show him a group of objects, and say, "Pick up the ball," the patient can do it. He can recognize meaning, but cannot produce speech. We also find that without grammar, understanding soon falters. A split-brain patient's right hemisphere cannot construct chunks, and as with R. H., complicated instructions soon overwhelm him. People whose interpretive memory no longer uses grammatical associations resemble patients who have lost the coordinated use of their brain and must rely on the silent right hemisphere.

Lost Meaning

Some people with dementia can read whole pages aloud, pronouncing the words correctly and maintaining the basic rhythms of speech, but they have no notion of what the words mean. They are like amateur performers singing an Italian aria nicely enough, but without a clue about their song's meaning.

These problems seemed so strange and so foreign to our theories of understanding that until recently we barely knew how to describe them, let alone analyze or explain them. Only in the past few decades have people gotten a serious model of complex actions without understanding. Computers do not know the meaning of words, and yet they can generate some sentences. The problems involved in programming computers to use language are exactly the problems facing a person who can no longer use the recognition side of a linguistic chunk. The machine has no purpose and no notion of where it is now.

Freud coined the name *agnosia,* meaning a state of not knowing, for the ruin of the recognition side of a chunk. It contrasts with *aphasia,* the usual term for people who cannot recall words and construct speech. We can understand the differences between the recall failures of aphasia and the broken recognition of agnosia by looking at the distinct problems these people have with words about color. In color aphasia a person cannot name a color, but can follow instructions about color. If you tell a color aphasic to pick up the red balloon, he can recognize the word *red* and pick up the appropriate balloon. But if you hand him the balloon and ask him what color it is, he cannot recall the name. In color agnosia a person cannot recognize the colors. A patient cannot follow instructions to pick the red balloon from a group of balloons.

The problems are interpretive. There is nothing wrong with the color aphasic's speech organs that blocks him from shaping the word with his mouth. Indeed he can make the same sound in other contexts, saying for example, "I *read* that book." The color agnosic's problem is also interpretive. There is nothing wrong with his eyes, nor is he color blind. Color aphasics can continue to use colors as reminders on lower levels of memory. For instance, a color aphasic could learn to select a red balloon to receive a piece of candy. This latter task relies simply on emotional memory (perceive color—evaluate as good to select). Selecting a color and receiving a reward is the sort of task Skinner proved repeatedly that even pigeons can learn. But when we ask someone to select a red balloon, emotional evaluations no longer matter. Now the person must associate the symbol with perceptions.

When the problem concerns something as ordinary as colors, the difficulties of a color agnosic seem unspeakably bizarre. Suppose instead of a pile of colored balloons we had a string of forty binary digits, as in the chunking experiment that George Miller described. We ask a person to pick out the pair of digits equal to the number three:

0110000110111010100001011001100010010101

Many people cannot accomplish the task, although with practice they could learn. Even without practice in binary numbers, however, most of us could learn quickly to select a billiard ball marked "11" and receive a reward. To a color agnosic, colors are as devoid of meaning as strings of binary digits.

Agnosia is an inability to interpret a perception. Often the problems take subtle and specific forms. In facial agnosia—the inability to recognize faces—a person might greet an old friend by saying, "How do you do, I'm so-and-so," and then be startled to hear a familiar voice reply, "Yes, dear. I know." The agnosic can still recognize voices. The oddity of such behavior seems to be increased by the survival of other levels of memory. When I see a good friend, I know who it is (interpretive memory) and feel affection (emotional memory). If the interpretive memory disappeared, the emotion would persist. I would feel the attraction and might want to introduce myself, to learn who this intriguing person is. So I would perpetually introduce myself to friends while continuing to ignore strangers.

In facial agnosia some people cannot recognize their own face in a mirror; it is perhaps the most bizarre agnosia of all. The notion of oneself does not disappear, but the connection between that idea and the face in the mirror has gone.

Not all agnosias concern visual perception. In anosognosia a person cannot recognize the fact that he is ill. He feels lousy, acts sick and rundown, but cannot make the leap from the symptoms to the perception, "I'm sick." There are also numerous agnosias for sounds. The most damaging such agnosia, an inability to recognize speech, is sometimes called word deafness because the patient reacts to other sounds, but treats language as empty noise. Some children are word deaf. Because they cannot recognize speech, they naturally never learn to use it. One study found that these children were just as willing to watch television with a garbled soundtrack as one with a clear track.

We recognize so much that we never think about the need for memory in such a task. Recognizing one's own illness seems no more than a sensory event. A person feels awful, so he knows he is sick. But of course we know that children often do not realize they are sick. Their parents recognize the symptoms before they do. Similarly, mature adults who have not been seriously ill for years may respond to a sudden disease more with confusion than recognition. Even the most basic experiences require remembering as well as sensation before a person can interpret what he sees.

A general agnosia lay behind Oliver Sacks's famous case of the "man who mistook his wife for a hat." The patient in this case, called Dr. P, could not recognize his hat, wife, or anything else. At one point the examining doctor handed Dr. P an object and asked what it was. Dr. P could see the thing perfectly and described it as "a continuous surface, infolded on itself. It appears to have five outpouchings, if this is the word." But for all his advanced geometry, P could not name the object.

Failure to name something often indicates a problem of recall, an inability to construct a word. Here, however, Dr. P's problem lay in an inability to know what word to construct. Like all patients with damaged interpretive memories he could not remember purposes and so could not imagine a use for the thing held in his hand. Dr. P did finally name the test item when, by chance, he slipped it on his hand and said, "My God, it's a glove." Only after he saw its purpose could be identify the strange object. We with our functioning memories move easily between present state and remembered purpose, but Dr. P was tied to the logic of his senses.

Missing Insights

Inborn problems in interpretive memory result in a failure to achieve insight, but of course years may pass before even the most basic problems become apparent. Often difficulties do not appear until school, and probably many people pass their whole lives without anyone realizing that a specific problem exists. We all know people without any spatial, or mechanical, or musical imagination. Does its absence indicate a lack of interest, a lack of confidence, or some specific inability to construct memory's top level?

In linguistic development the earliest signs cannot appear before age three or four, the age at which most children begin to speak from interpretive memory. Language development studies have reported the case of a preschooler called John whose speech at the age of three and one half reflected nothing beyond factual memory. John needed a physical reminder to talk about anything, including playful singing or chanting. Even if a parent began singing a familiar song, John still needed a tangible reminder to join in. To sing something like the eeyi-eeyi-o chorus in Old Macdonald, John would have to have a toy associated with the past experience of singing the chorus. The words by themselves were not enough. When he played with his toys he talked, but almost every word he spoke was an exact quotation of something he had heard. He never had any insights that let him modify his speech to suit the situation. As with normal children, his speech grew longer. He went from one-word expressions like "mama," to two, "mama come," to three, "mama come chair." As sentences grow longer, however, they become increasingly unintelligible if not supported by grammar. John could stick more words together, one behind the other, but they never took on grammatical order and never served any communicative purposes. The insights that transform clichés into appropriate speech never came.

Fortunately, such dramatic problems are rare. Children usually learn to talk without needing much help. Reading problems, however, are widespread. Our powers of speech are instinctive throughout the species, but reading is a cultural adaptation and we should not expect the genes that support reading to be so universal. Inborn reading problems are called *dyslexia*. At one time dyslexia was thought rare and attributed solely to difficulties in perception. Recent work has found that the problem is more common than once supposed and there are many types of dyslexia.

No one has yet made a detailed comparison of the workings of memory and the forms of dyslexia; however, many of the problems do match what the memory staircase leads us to expect. Attentional dyslexia, for example, is an inability to pay attention to a specific letter in a group of letters. If we show one letter to a child with attentional dyslexia, he can name it, but if we show the child the same letter surrounded by other letters he has a much harder time. With an inability to attend to specific letters in a string, a child's reading can stumble even before reaching the level of factual memory.

Some children with good powers of attention can develop problems based on a poor prompt recall for written words. Although we understand sentences as unified chunks, we encounter their parts sequentially and must remember the parts individually before perceiving their meaning. This need for memory probably puts limits on everybody's reading and listening abilities. Consider a sentence like:

> When verbose Victor grew silent, John, the honest, honored, once-famous, long-feared, grey-bearded, dandified old gentleman who had so impressed the electorate of all Alabama, rose like a pitiful, tired, bankrupt, bedraggled refugee from Troy to begin speaking pleadingly with the six bored voters of Lee's Crossing.

This sentence has so many lists of details that readers forget they are reading about John, let alone his characteristics. In dyslexic cases powers of prompt recall for written words may be so weak that people can have trouble understanding even short sentences. They may find trouble even with a sentence like:

Spot ran up the stairs.

In this sentence, *Spot* is a dog's name and understanding it requires no memory for the rest of the sentence. Understanding *ran* takes a little more memory. The reader must remember that Spot is running. Understanding *up* puts yet more of a strain on memory. The reader must remember first that Spot ran and then must wait for the word *stairs* to learn what he ran up. A person with limited prompt recall for written words can have trouble remembering a word's context, and recognition depends on context. In cases of reading students diagnosed as suffering from deep dyslexia the students find it easiest to read nouns like *Spot,* and hardest to read prepositions like *up*. With such a troubled factual memory, a reading student cannot easily advance to reading on memory's interpretive level.

These students make reading errors similar to the errors found in testing factual memory. In tests of factual memory a person might read the word *salt* on a list, and recall instead its common associate, *pepper*. Students whose reading is stuck on the factual level can make similar errors. They might see the word *merry* but speak its common associate *Christmas*. These errors indicate reading without understanding.

Even if factual memory is in good working order, a person may still have problems either recognizing or constructing words. Some people can construct written words, but not recognize them. They read by spelling the words, letter by letter, either silently or aloud. Often, these people can write and spell well, but they have a hard time reading what they wrote.

Other reading students have problems recalling written words. Instead of spelling them out, they must translate the letters into sounds and sound them out. This system works well for a word like *hat* but does not work for *knight*. These children often spell poorly, but phonetically.

It is difficult to read a list of dyslexia symptoms and not suspect that each of us has traces of at least some of its forms. Our improved understanding of genetics has led to the discovery of many more hereditary diseases. Our new understanding of memory seems equally likely to find many previously unsuspected imbalances in interpretation. In most cases there is probably no *right* balance. Different balances lead to different strengths, making one person an accountant, another a mathematician, and yet letting both find fulfillment in their work.

13

AMNESIA:

THE FAILURE OF FACTUAL MEMORY

And think no more of this night's accidents
But as the fierce vexation of a dream.

—Shakespeare, *A Midsummer Night's Dream*, c 1595

W hen reminders cease to trigger associations factual memory has broken down. The inability to learn new reminders is among the most common forms of pathological forgetting. It changes life from steady adaptation and learning to something much like an endless dream in which shadows pass without explanation or expectation. The general term for this breakdown is *amnesia*.

Popular dramatists and novelists have long used amnesia as a plot device. The hero or heroine receives a blow on the head and, upon coming to, cannot remember anything—except how to speak, chase bandits, make love, and do the other things no potboiler can do without. The amnesia lets the character move through an alien world and have new adventures before receiving another blow on the head and returning to a normal suburban life back in Milksop Heights. We have seen this story so often that people begin to assume it must have some basis; however, this species of amnesia, the forgetting of one's own history without losing any other faculties of mind, is a writer's invention. The closest thing to it in real life, known as a fugue, is an incident involving failure to use the emotional level of memory and we will discuss it in the next chapter. Although potboiler amnesia favors the forgetting of events that happened before the onset of the problem, real amnesia almost always destroys the ability to remember things that happen after the problem begins.

The ruin of factual memory also halts any further development of interpretive memory. A person can no longer have insights into his own experience. The most terribly wounded amnesics cannot achieve even the insight necessary for them to realize that they have amnesia. They live trapped in a world where experience does not improve their understanding. They cannot organize their experiences into new chunks and cannot describe any episodes in their life that happened after the onset of amnesia. Because it takes an insight into one's experiences to realize there is a problem, patients with amnesia are often completely unaware that their memory no longer works properly. They forget that they do not remember.

Although amnesiacs can no longer remember new facts long enough to construct new chunks, they do not forget their old chunks. Amnesia damages the functioning of factual memory, but does not destroy existing powers of interpretive memory. In contrast to one suffering from facial agnosia (a problem on the interpretive level), a person with amnesia will find that people become harder to recognize because they grow older and look less like the way the amnesiac remembers them. In contrast to one suffering from aphasia (another interpretive-level failure), an amnesiac often grows quiet for another reason. He has less and less to say. The amnesia appears to alienate him from his surroundings.

When amnesiacs do talk they often invent their facts. These fabrications are known as confabulation. Some amnesiacs confabulate extensively, telling stories about themselves and their activities. The stories rely on chunks established before the amnesia so the details sound plausible. A man will say that he played pool last night. He did not, but at one time in the past he played pool often. As the confabulations become longer, however, the speaker forgets the story he is telling. The confabulation becomes incoherent, taking on the characteristics of a dream in which setting and situation are liable to change in an instant.

Factual memory helps keep normal people from slipping into incoherence by using the steady presence of orienting reminders. We take our orientation for granted and do not ask how we know where we are, but we are surrounded by reminders that evoke and provide associations that connect us to our present. These reminders and their associations also serve to keep us up to date. For example, if your child marries, you must remember this new detail. If your car is stolen, you must not plan to use it this evening. The continual learning of new facts and the extinction of old ones is a part of every normal life. With amnesiacs that process disappears. The old stays learned, the new remains foreign. As time passes, less and less knowledge remains current. People grow older and less recognizable. Neighborhoods, prices, and social values change. Television programs come and go, and so do public officials. Amnesiacs sometimes seem to live in the past, because they cannot remember anything that happened since some distant time, however their nonorientation makes it hard to say they live in any time. They are lost in timelessness.

Many of the symptoms of amnesia appear to be symptoms of a massive disorientation. Amnesiacs often seem alert and attentive, but their actions, like their stories, become incoherent. They appear motivated, but cannot sustain an activity. Their behavior is reminiscent of the brain-damaged woman who could no longer fillet fish, but the basis of the unproductive activity is not quite the same. For amnesiacs, the problem lies in sustaining attention for a task. An amnesiac who learned chess before the onset of his memory problem, for example, can still remember the purpose of chess and can talk about chess positions. He may even start to play a game, but as the match continues he forgets what he is doing. To continue playing he must keep his attention on the board. The board itself shows the current position, and in theory, an amnesiac might not need to remember the game so far if he could analyze the position. After all, computers play chess without remembering how a position arose, but computers do not depend on attention. Normal chess players are sometimes distracted, but can return their attention to the game. Distracted amnesiacs forget the game exists. A normal chess player sees the position and remembers how it came to be. These associations help sustain a player's interest, reminding him of the struggle that has already taken place on the board and of any little strategic ambitions he may cherish. Without these associations to help sustain interest in the game, the activity of playing chess peters out. Apparently orientation is as important as purpose in prolonged action.

People who suffer from transient amnesias because of blows on the head or epileptic seizures often speak of the terrifying disorientation. After a seizure, epileptics are disoriented and have no memory of the incident. They need to be told: It is all right; you have had a seizure, but it passed; now you are at such and such a place. I know the disorientation of amnesia from personal experience. I was once in a motorcycle accident in which I banged my head. Fortunately, I wore a helmet, and apart from a scar on my chin, the damage was extremely short-lived, but for perhaps an hour I was as disoriented and confused as I ever hope to be. I forgot everything. I did not remember the accident or the people who stopped to help or that I was on my way to a clinic. I was not unconscious, just confused. Even now, I can recall only one image from that blackout period. I am on the front seat of a Land-Rover beside a man taking me to a clinic. The grey metal dashboard rattles in front of me. The strong brown arms of the driver emerge from white sleeves and hold the steering wheel. I am thinking, "What is happening? Why don't I know what is happening?" and I am terrified, as terrified as I have ever been. I am not afraid of what will happen or what these people in the Land-Rover might intend. I have no thoughts about that. It is the complete alienation between myself and my surroundings that terrifies me. That terrified arousal probably explains why I can remember this single moment. For years after this event I wrote stories that began with characters suddenly coming to, with no knowledge or sense of where they were or how they came to be there.

Even if an amnesiac's disorientation does not alarm him, its terrible consequences distinguish amnesia from ordinary cases of poor memory. Reminders may not remind us of much for long, but we do know where we are. Factual recall depends on the richness of its associations. Some experiences have so many associations that many events can remind us of them. This process of acquiring associations, known technically as memory consolidation, can persist for years. If they form few associations with a particular experience, ordinary people in perfect health forget about the event. In this sense, amnesia for most things is routine. Yet, a precise reminder can suddenly trigger old associations in normal people. They can visit a place they have not seen or thought of in years, and suddenly remember particular associations from decades ago.

Deliberate Cases

Since attention raises us to the factual memory level, memory falters when attention falters. In theory, serious brain damage could destroy a person's ability to pay attention to anything, but in practice that problem seems unknown (unless this is the brain damage that underlies autism). Voluntary inattention, however, is common. People can decide that happiness does not lie in a particular direction, and look away. We can see this phenomenon in movie theaters as audience members deliberately turn away from some approaching screen violence. These refusals show the intricacy of the memory staircase. A memory level can be damaged objectively by a disruption in the brain circuitry, or subjectively by its simply not being used. In the case of factual memory we can develop amnesia for specific experiences by deciding to stop our construction one step down, on the emotional level. This form of amnesia is commonly referred to as a repressed memory.

Because repression is an emotional response to a particular event, it has proven difficult to study under laboratory conditions, but a recent experiment managed to create memory repression. Subjects looked at slides of faces. Each slide listed four brief descriptions of the person shown. Before viewing the slides, the subjects received a shot of adrenalin. As we might expect, their memories for the faces and the descriptions were good. The subjects were aroused but not alarmed, and they paid good attention to what they saw. A second group viewed the same slides but became aroused in a different manner. They too received an injection, but it was merely a salty solution with no arousal effect. The real arousal came when in the course of the slide show the subjects suddenly saw a series of horrifying images that raised their emotional reactions. Researchers then tested memory by showing the faces from the slides and asking the subjects to recall the associated descriptions. Not surprisingly, the emotionally aroused group did not do as well as the group aroused through adrenalin shots.

The subjects were attached to devices similar to lie detectors to measure their physiologic responses to the slides, and by that measure both groups were equally aroused. Both groups also completed questionnaires about their reactions, and that test also scored the two groups as having similar levels of arousal. So, by available standards, the two groups appeared to have been equally aroused, but one group's memory was better. Despite the fact that the experiment contains ambiguities and the techniques used to measure arousal are far from perfect, the results suggest the effects of repression. Traumatic arousal leads to uncertain memories. Memory depends on active efforts at construction. We have to pay attention to learn and pay attention again to remember. We may not construct memories associated with awful things as well as we construct other memories. We should not expect emotional memory to encourage that pursuit up to the level of factual memory. Even without pathological amnesia, we can feel reluctant to remember.

The theory of deliberate repression of memory is Freud's most famous contribution to memory studies. He considered repression the keystone of his entire theory of neurosis; there is, however, an important difference between refusing to climb to memory's higher levels and the older idea of repressing a memory. Freud took it for granted that all memories are stored somewhere in the brain and that we automatically retrieve these memories when we need them. In his clinical work, however, he constantly saw people who could not remember important things. What, he asked, caused this failure of retrieval? He assumed there must be some active but unknown agent repressing the memory.

Freud's observation of deliberate amnesia was an accurate and original contribution to memory theory, but his belief in storage was misplaced. The memory staircase provides a different explanation. At the level of emotional memory, decisions depend on a basic recognition that leaves us feeling attraction, repulsion, curiosity, or boredom. Because we respond from Proustian recognition alone, we do not know the historical basis for our emotion. We have seen before that it takes courage to climb to memory's higher levels. If an emotional association is particularly frightening or one's temperament is timid, a person can halt at memory's emotional level and remember no more. Deliberate refusal resembles habituation. At the levels of factual memory, habituation begins as a decision that something is not worth attending to. Emotional refusal too begins as a decision that the consequences of attending to something are too disagreeable to pursue.

The older theory assumed that if we could overcome a block to memory, we would automatically remember and—if the block had really been overcome—the memory would be accurate. The theory of refusal is less encouraging. We may summon the courage and strength to try to remember, but the effort does not guarantee success, especially for memories that we have refused to think of for years. We cannot assume that our memory will be historically correct when at last we recall some long-refused fact. Everything we have learned about memory suggests that the result will mix fact and fiction into a compound beyond sorting. If we deliberately refuse to remember an episode, we can suffer (or enjoy) a lifetime's amnesia for the event.

Case of K. F.'s Motorcycle Accident

We can form factual associations as a result of a double take as well as because of immediate arousal. Some forms of brain damage can damage the power of prompt recall. The orientation reaction survives, but a person cannot make the double take that should let him pay attention to something he originally ignored. The first person studied with this problem is known as patient K. F. The case was reported in 1969 by a pair of British researchers, Elizabeth Warrington and Tim Shallice.

K. F. suffered brain damage in a motorcycle accident. Generally, he does well, but the accident almost destroyed his prompt recall of sounds. Tests show a recency effect for auditory stimuli of only one item. If he hears a string of two digits—say 6, 3—he can recall only the 3. He has already forgotten the 6. Although serious, it is not a ruinous problem; only when life gets complicated does K. F. exhibit the disorientation that comes from damaged prompt recall. A number of tests were given in order to examine this problem. An example of such a study is in the use of plastic cutouts—triangles, squares, and circles of various sizes and colors. If an examiner said, "Touch the large green circle," K. F. could do it. He could also follow instructions if they were given in sequence, as in, "Take the small red triangle and touch it against the large green circle." Apparently he could organize these instructions into a chunk and use them. But if examiners gave these same instructions in reverse sequence—"Touch the large green circle with the small red triangle"—K. F. could not follow them. A close look at that sentence shows us where K. F.'s problem lies. Simple as the sentence seems, it requires prompt recall. The first item (large green circle) depends on the second item (small red triangle). K. F. can pick up the triangle, but by then he has forgotten what he should do with it. When he was first diagnosed, his case seemed unique. Since then, several similar cases have appeared.

Because prompt recall is only one basis for developing factual associations, this form of brain damage does not lead to complete amnesia. K. F. likes to follow current events and can discuss the latest news. Often he seems perfectly normal, but then someone recites something like a phone number and his shaky grip on reality becomes apparent. He forgets the number as it is still being spoken.

Case of H. M.'s Surgery

We have already mentioned the most notorious case of amnesia in memory studies, the story of patient H. M. In 1953, H. M. underwent radical brain surgery to treat epilepsy. Following the operation he never again learned a new association. By terrible misjudgment, the surgeon had destroyed both of H. M.'s hippocampuses, exactly those parts of the brain necessary to form new factual associations. It is as though the operation had sliced through the memory staircase at the factual level. Everything below the slice continues to function; nothing has appeared above the cut. H. M. continues to enjoy a good memory for the details of his life up until three weeks before the operation. And because the surgery did not damage his powers of attention, he continues to orient toward surprises and tests show normal prompt recall.

Because of the precision of the damage, H. M.'s is the most closely studied case in the history of amnesia. It established positively that past reminders continue to function in amnesia, but that amnesia destroys the ability to learn new reminders. The forgetting of the three weeks before the brain damage is called retrograde (or retroactive) amnesia. Amnesiacs usually do suffer some forgetting of associations that preceded the injury, although often it is mild. An old speculation, known as Ribot's conjecture, holds that retrograde amnesia affects older memories less than memories for events that occurred just before the injury. The conjecture is unproven, but widely supported by clinical observation. Doctors used to consider retrograde amnesia as a loss of stored memories. That explanation began to falter as more and more cases showed spontaneous recovery and rapid reversal. The victims could not recover from the amnesia if they really stored memories and the stores had really been lost.

Amnesia appears to disrupt the brain's capacity to change its circuitry and form new factual associations. Thus, amnesiacs cannot recall new experiences after a trauma because they form no associations with the context of those experiences. At the same time, experiences immediately before the trauma may still have so few associations that nothing reminds an amnesiac of them. An analysis of retrograde amnesia published in 1984 found that it is indeed a failure of cues and that the more severe the amnesia the farther back in time the retrograde amnesia extends. Throughout our lives we add new associations to some old memories, associating them with later occasions when we were reminded of them. It seems more like a process of enriching than of congealing or consolidating. Retrograde amnesia affects those associations that time has not yet enriched sufficiently. Sometimes in the general blank of retrograde amnesia a person will have an island of recollection about a particularly important event.

One of the most startling findings about H. M. turned up a significant improvement in IQ. Before the operation his intelligence was normal but undistinguished, almost perfectly average. Tests after the operation scored him in the top third of the population. Few discoveries could more profoundly challenge the assumptions that underlie measures of intelligence, for H. M. can barely function. He is so disoriented, so unable to learn the most basic associations, that a person who did not know his history would conclude that H. M. was probably the least intelligent fellow he had ever met. Yet his IQ score went up.

Intelligence tests deliberately avoid measuring the concrete knowledge that comes with experience. Recognition and reminders are exactly what the test authors try not to measure because one person may not have had the experience to know particular facts or recognize particular things. (No IQ test has ever successfully abolished all questions that call for concrete knowledge.) IQ tests challenge a person's ability to use grammatical associations and generalized facts. Amnesiacs retain their ability to use previously established grammatical associations and their generalized knowledge continues to grow.

We saw that generalized learning comes when we do not pay attention to the context of an experience. For example, if I had not paid so much attention to the situation in which I learned the word *punctual,* its meaning for me would be more general. Tests have shown that amnesiacs have nearly normal abilities to learn details without an explicit context. Some studies have tested the capacity of amnesiacs to remember words from lists. During recall they are as likely to remember a word from an earlier list as from the list they have just heard. This same phenomenon accompanies generalized learning in normal people.

Tests of amnesiac recognition do show a general bias toward past experience, but with no memory for the details of the experience. Experimenters presented subjects with a list and afterward forced the subjects to study word pairs and choose between the two words, guessing which word they saw before. Under these conditions, amnesiacs will recognize a word from the studied list almost as reliably as normal subjects, but the amnesiacs do not remember the learning episode; they just know.

H. M. has learned things since 1953, but he has no idea how he knows them. He also shows good motor memory. As we have seen, motor memory, like learning to ride a bicycle, is so basic that even butterflies can use it. We saw that babies use it to suck their thumbs, so we would not expect damage high up the staircase to disrupt it. H. M.'s still survives. He has learned a so-called stylus maze, a maze that one explores with a pointer. The explorer cannot see the maze, but simply examines it by feel. Learning depends on motor memory. H. M. experimented with such a maze several times. Each time he protested that he had never seen the maze before, and yet he improved. Finally, he could put a pointer in the maze and move it directly to the exit point without making an error, objecting all the while that he had never touched the maze before and could not possibly solve it.

Alcoholic Cases

Long-term amnesias can have many causes, including a thiamin deficiency (usually associated with alcoholism), prolonged lack of oxygen (sometimes following a heart attack), and a severe blow to the head. The most widely studied form of amnesia comes from alcoholism and is known as Korsakoff's syndrome. The worst cases are sometimes called Korsakoff's psychosis. It is a progressive disease, and the extent of its damage varies. Even short bouts of drunkenness can leave a person amnesic for the period of intoxication, and patients with Korsakoff's syndrome usually suffer from a retrograde amnesia more severe than the three-week loss of patient H. M.

Many of their symptoms match those of H. M. They are perpetually disoriented. Usually their disease forces them to live in a hospital. Since they came to the hospital after the amnesia began, they have no memory of being in a hospital or knowledge of why they are there. They do not recognize their doctors or nurses, even after years of care. At the same time, as a mercy from generalized memory, the hospital setting comes to seem vaguely familiar, so their disorientation is more dreamlike than frightening. They almost always confabulate, sometimes incessantly, as they invent an incoherent world in which the present reminds them only of places and people long past.

Emotional memory continues to function in amnesiac patients. A French psychologist, Edouard Claparède, performed an experiment in 1911 on a woman with Korsakoff's syndrome. He hid a pin in his fingers, reached for her hand, and stuck her. Later, he again reached toward her hand, and she pulled her hand back. Claparède pressed her for an explanation of the withdrawn hand. She, of course, could not remember the fact of having been stuck, but the Proustian recognition of potential pain survived. The best explanation the woman could provide for her behavior was a generalized remark: "Sometimes pins are hidden in people's hands."

In his book, *The Man Who Mistook His Wife for a Hat,* Oliver Sacks tells of a patient with Korsakoff's syndrome who, while living in the 1980s, could remember nothing he had learned since 1945. Yet he formed a powerful new emotional relationship with his brother. Although dead to new facts, his emotional memory continued to develop, permitting experiences and behavior unknown to the man in 1945.

The survival of emotional memory in amnesia is exactly what the memory staircase leads us to expect. In many ways, amnesia reduces a person to intellectual infancy. He lives and learns as a baby does. One 1985 article on amnesia noted, "The memory tests in which infants [up to about their first birthday] succeeded were similar to those on which amnesic patients demonstrated preserved mental abilities, whereas those tests on which infants failed, amnesic patients also displayed a profound impairment." But these people are not children, and they do not outgrow the limits of their memories.

14

FORGETTING

TO REMEMBER:

THE FAILURE OF
EMOTIONAL MEMORY

This counsel [to "know thyself"] has been often given
with serious dignity, and often received with appearance
of conviction; but as very few can search deep into their
own minds without meeting what they wish to hide from
themselves, scarce any man persists in cultivating such
disagreeable acquaintance, but draws the veil again between his eyes and his heart, leaves his passions and
appetites as he found them, and advises others to look
into themselves.

—Samuel Johnson, *The Idler* #27, 1758

When children construct levels of memory, they
come more profoundly into contact with the world beyond their
skins. Forgetting retreats from that contact. Even ordinary
forgetting is a transitory slipping of the grip. That sense of
alienation from the truth of things makes absentmindedness so
frustrating. It adds a sense of incompetence to an already
irritating confusion. The sight of pathological forgetting is even
more terrifying because we can see a person has lost hold of

something real. Creative understanding disappears when one forgets chunks; factual associations go next, leaving a person with only emotional memory. At that level one can still learn, still form and develop emotional bonds with the world. When emotional memory fails too, contact with reality ends.

Physical brain damage that destroys emotional memory would be so devastating that it is hard to imagine. A person would either be comatose or so retarded as to be nearly immobile. Thus, the only examples we can study of people who forgo their emotional memory are neurotics. When they reject the use of emotional memory, they are really trying to reject themselves and the world. People who have abandoned emotional memory might no longer turn their noses from the smell of ammonia or might even prefer to bark like a dog rather than speak English.

Bizarre as these responses sound, they have become a familiar part of the folklore. We treat hypnotism's strange powers as a scientifically mystical way to "refresh" memory, or as light entertainment. We could just as easily consider them as warnings. When the stage hypnotist tells a person, "I am going to hand you a bouquet of roses," the audience laughs as the subject takes a rag soaked in ammonia and sniffs it deeply, as though finding pleasure. If a stolid banker appears on stage and barks like a dog or a large man acts like a seductive woman, the audience treats it as mere amusement. Stage hypnotism should not be taken seriously, we feel.

If the same act were performed in another spirit, however, it could be terrifying. I once watched an African magician demonstrate hypnotism and nobody laughed. The performance was simple, yet its point was super-serious: We can lose contact with the world in an instant. The magician asked his audience of students to nominate a "volunteer" for the demonstration, and a boy was sent forward. He grinned a little sheepishly as his friends laughed and stirred in their seats. The magician sat the boy on a table and the student's eyes suddenly lost their sparkle, for no clear reason that I could see. The magician was talking, giving instructions too quickly for me to follow. The boy began to slip backward until he was lying immobile on the table. The magician continued his talk, now directing it toward the audience, and at first most people paid more attention to him than to the student who lay on the table. But slowly eyes shifted to the boy. I was a little puzzled. I expected more from a display of hypnotism. Some of the audience called to their friend; no reply. Slowly the cumulative strangeness of the scene began to affect me. The boy did nothing and I thought, well, do something. And he did nothing. The magician babbled on about the mystery of hypnotism, and the boy still did nothing. More time, more nothing. And still nothing until finally it sank in: He is going to do nothing. The boy was gone, out of touch. He could lie there forever like a corpse at a wake. The noise, the heat, and the presence of friends had lost their hold on him.

To recall his subject to life the hypnotist blew cigarette smoke in his face. The boy jerked up, and then stumbled back to his classmates with a walk as unsteady as Lazarus's after his time in the tomb. Only when I saw the stupor in the face of the boy returning to his seat did I know for sure that he had not been faking. Somehow, without any apparent effort, he had been transformed from grinning student into a totally disoriented boy.

Sometimes people can abolish their own orientation through self-hypnotism. They suggest to themselves that the world is other than it is, and memory tumbles. They may suggest to themselves a new identity. Self-hypnotism on this level seldom turns a person into a barking dog, but it changes the way he responds to perceptions. The most familiar examples of this form of change come during play. A child who is normally frightened of people in costume, may—when in a scary Halloween costume of his own—suddenly assume the identity suggested by his dress and roar back at witches and goblins. Or self-hypnotism can suggest that unwanted perceptions do not exist. In ordinary experience we call these withdrawals daydreaming. Bored students imagine a world of their own and many a television viewer steps into a private fantasy as soon as the commercials begin. Paradoxically, then, the destruction of all memory begins with a decision at memory's highest level that the world and oneself are no longer compatible. A person wishes the world were some other way, and changes that wish into experience. Recognition disappears; hallucinations begin.

Societies have recognized the symptoms of such break-downs for thousands of years and diagnosed them variously as devil possession, malingering, laziness, self-pity, cowardice, lack of will, obstinacy, contrariness, and irresponsibility. The list does not show much sympathy for the sufferer; devil possession is the least judgmental diagnosis of the lot. A breakdown this profound can signal memory's complete failure. Memory can no longer use a person's desires and understanding to answer the question, "What should I do now?"

Society always limits its members' freedom, and sometimes it tells them precisely what they must do. This power leads to the tensions between duty and desire, between the group and the individual, that characterize every society. Sometimes this tension becomes so overpowering that a person abandons memory altogether. The people most likely to suffer this final memory loss, naturally, are the ones most constrained and channeled by society—notably women, dependent children old enough to know their own minds, soldiers, and minority groups. Although I normally praise the orienting powers of the higher memory levels, orientation may not seem desirable if life and the world become a nightmare.

Suppose, for example, you are a soldier about to go over the top in a charge against enemy machine guns. You probably do not want to go, but your sergeant and your pride say you must. Under such pressure, you might forget the identity that entraps you and start to flee. This breakdown is as close as forgetting ever gets to potboiler amnesia, but in books and movies these incidents usually begin with a blow to the head. In real life they begin with the rejection of self and circumstance. The technical name for this kind of forgetting is *fugue*, meaning flight, because along with the loss of identity, a person desperately wants to go somewhere else. Often people in a fugue discover they have forgotten their identity only when somebody asks them for their name and they realize that they do not know it.

Most fugues are short lived, lasting no more than a few hours, and they often have some element of absurdly inappropriate behavior about them. In one such case, a woman called I. J. was at a party with her husband. She enjoyed it because the gathering had many men who flirted with her, but she reluctantly left when her husband said they must. They were visitors in town, and back at the hotel I. J. entered a fugue state. She returned to the hotel lobby and was picked up by another guest. In his room they had intercourse numerous times, and during the whole interlude I. J. talked about the weather. Her husband had once advised her that if a man tried to pick her up she should talk about the weather.

In another case a fugue lasted for perhaps only an hour. In this incident a light-skinned black called C. D. was visiting a city where he bumped into a white friend and his white girl friend. One of the men suggested they go horseback riding, but the girl objected, saying she would not ride with a Creole. C. D. was stung to the quick, but he remembered a lynching he had witnessed and said nothing. Instead he briefly entered a fugue state in which he was completely at a loss to know who or where he was.

Fugue is probably most common among soldiers in or bound for combat. During World War II 5 percent of American neuropsychiatric patients in the South Pacific suffered from it. One case of unusually long duration lasted thirty-two days. A soldier, known as A. B. in the case studies, was on a raiding party in Africa when a German dive bomber came straight toward him. A. B. should have fired at the plane, but his hand froze on the gun. He thought to himself, "I can't take it. I have to get out of here. I'm yellow. I'm a coward." The next thing he knew he was in a hospital in Syria hundreds of miles to the east and somebody was asking him his name. In his fugue he had fled far from the scene of battle. A. B. had almost no memory for those days of escape, but while in the hospital he himself likened his fugue state to being hypnotized.

The Fugue of Louise L.

Fugues are usually only partial. A person wants to flee and forgets one identity, but does not replace it with a new one. Recently, however, a military doctor reported an unusually complete fugue case in which the patient, Louise L., did invent a new identity. This exchange permitted Louise a range of astonishing accomplishments as she took both the name and talents of her new persona. Louise had, in effect, hypnotized herself and given herself a new set of skills. After her fugue a psychiatrist gave Louise a battery of tests. Measuring hypnotizability on a scale from 1 to 5, she scored a 5.

Louise was a teenage girl trapped in an unhappy situation. Her parents had recently divorced, and during that process she had five or six hallucinations in which she saw her mother lying in a pool of blood. Once during a hallucination Louise began screaming in the middle of class. Her mother married an enlisted man and Louise disapproved. After the marriage, Louise had several fainting spells in school. The family was then transferred to a remote overseas military post. While she was living in this isolated area Louise underwent her extraordinary fugue.

It began with an especially unhappy experience at a school dance. The school French Club organized a kissing booth, and Louise joined in the project; the other girls then left her alone in the booth. To add more humiliation to her loneliness, almost nobody bought a kiss from her. The next night, after a picnic, Louise, her sister, and a girlfriend went for a walk. They met two boys and the other girls abandoned Louise to go off with them. Not knowing what to do, Louise climbed a tree and wished to heaven she could be somewhere else. Later she reported that while up in the tree she said to herself, "I am going to leave this place. I don't know how, but I will, and I'm not going to come back until I have healed the hurt and until people realize I have feelings. I am not a nobody, a marionette on a stage." As she grew more angry she remembered a nightmare she had had of a French woman trapped in a burning pioneer's cabin. Recalling the dream, Louise said to the woman, "Take my place."

When Louise came down from the tree she was in a stupor. Her sister got her home in a taxi. Louise did not recognize her family; she spoke mainly French and her English had a heavy French accent. She claimed to be Jeanne Marie Theresa Le Grand Ducourtieux, and she was determined to go to Marietta, Ohio, to join her husband. She thought the date was some time around 1803, and she did not use words or facts that post-dated that era.

The fugue lasted for several days, and during that time Louise's family had to actively keep her from trying to get to Marietta. "Jeanne" disliked the modern clothes she wore and sewed herself a sun bonnet and a long calico skirt. She cooked ham and French pastry for her amazed family. Previously, Louise had failed even to sew buttons on straight, and her parents also considered cooking beyond her. Her new abilities probably resulted from sudden attention. Louise could not be bothered to sew or cook well, but "Jeanne" concentrated on her task. The French she spoke was less astounding. She had studied it since fourth grade and was active in the French Club.

William James said fugues were trances of unusually long duration, and we have learned nothing to question his opinion. Louise's hypnotic susceptibility and her deliberate decision to abandon her identity argue that she replaced recognition with a world of her own suggestion. Surely the most surprising part of "Jeanne's" behavior was her acquisition of new skills. It suggests that people have a potential to do many things they never do. Because remembering is active, it can change if we suddenly pay attention to new things and ignore old distractions. With a change in ambition as drastic as that of Louise's fugue, it is as though a new person had taken over the memory levels.

Louise seems to have quit her fugue after less than a week because her mother had adapted to the change too well. Her mother acted as though she preferred having a hard-working helpful "Jeanne" around the house, and she showed no hint of awareness that her daughter's problem might indicate serious difficulties within the family. Louise found that she had become an unusually helpful daughter, and that result had not been the purpose of her attempted escape.

The Hysteria of Anna O.

An even more debilitating self-hypnosis leads to lost perception, hallucination, and inability to function. It is commonly called hysteria. In ordinary speech, the term usually means no more than an overly emotional or fearful reaction. In psychiatric history's classic cases, hysteria substitutes suggestion for recognition. Instead of wanting to flee, hysterics may become nearly immobile.

A famous case in psychiatric literature is the hysteria of a young Viennese woman named Bertha Pappenheim, referred to by Sigmund Freud and his colleague Joseph Breuer as Anna O. Anna became Breuer's patient in 1880. Freud learned of her case only after the fact, but it led him to the technique of letting patients talk about their problems.

As with Louise L., Anna O., was highly hypnotizable. During her years of treatment Breuer hypnotized her on an almost daily basis for hours at a time and she seems to have excelled at self-hypnosis too. Before the onset of her hysteria she had systematically hallucinated an alternate world that she called her "private theater." Anna lived in a fairy-tale domain of her own imagination and might have moved forever into a dream world, like one of Tennessee Williams's southern belles, had her father not, in July 1880, become fatally ill with tuberculosis. Anna and her mother shared nursing duties, and it became essential that Anna stay alert and tend to the invalid.

Anna's life bore certain thematic resemblances to Louise's. Both were trapped in situations where memory served only to remind them of their prison. Louise was young and lived with her family on a remote island. Anna was older than Louise (twenty-one), and today there would be no question about such a bright, capable woman going off to seek her fortune, but the Vienna of her day expected complete self-denial from women. Anna's life rested on duty, and she refused ever to show emotion. She spent her days tending to her dying father, never giving way to anger, refusing even to let her father see her tears. Anna seems to have found no relief, no soldier's night off to unwind and laugh about respected superiors. Nor did she try to personalize her duty, to change it to desire. It is possible to tend to a dying person with love and even to find pleasure in the intimacy it brings, but Anna did not understand duty that way. She seems to have viewed it as a substitute for her own desires. If left to choose for herself, she would have developed in other ways, but she was not left to choose. She accepted her fate, although privately she was miserable about not having her own way. Thirty years later, looking back on this period, she wrote in a letter, "How happy are present-day girls! I remember how difficult people made it for me at this age trying to keep me from the way that was right for me." Yet for all her resentment, Anna did not rebel—not overtly at any rate.

The illness of her father brought Anna's impotence to a crisis. It took all her time and concentration to attend to him. She could no longer retreat into her private theater, but she could not bear her new life either. Her first reported symptom of the change was an hysterical cough. Once while ministering to her father she heard an orchestra playing in a house across the way. Anna briefly wished she could be at the party, and then felt guilty for wanting to dance while her father lay in such a state. She coughed instead, and from then on, she coughed whenever she heard music.

This little change typified the way Anna altered her emotional memory. She heard music—perhaps one of Johann Strauss's new waltzes—and associated the music with happiness. As her thoughts climbed the memory levels, she remembered her father and her duty and she despised her wish for fun. Her self-contempt changed the association she had with music:

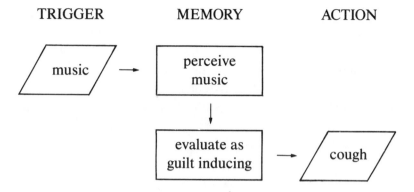

TRIGGER   MEMORY   ACTION

Because she evaluated so many things as guilt inducing, she was prone to continual nervous coughing.

Finally, in December, after half a year of this duty, Anna took to her bed. She did not live in the constant deep trance of Louise L. Instead, Anna flickered between memory and suggestion. When she used some memory, Anna was much her usual self except that she stayed in bed and had a bag of bizarre behaviors, like coughing at the sound of music, revulsion at the sight of water, and speaking only in English. During her loathing of water she survived only by eating fruits, and her use of English forced the Viennese family to hire an English-speaking governess. When suggestion took over completely Anna lost her powers of recognition and even perception. When her recognition powers failed, she did not see people and did not hear them. Dr. Breuer managed to break through to her and could maintain contact by steady speech, but Anna did not perceive strangers. Once Breuer brought a colleague to observe her, and she literally did not see the man. She discovered the second doctor only when, like my African magician, he blew cigar smoke in her face. She looked around to find the source of the smoke and suddenly saw the stranger. She began to run and fell unconscious onto the floor.

Anna O. eventually overcame her hysteria and became an important figure in Austria's feminist movement. Like Louise, she seems largely to have recovered on her own, although her changing circumstances surely helped. Her father died; she went into a sanitarium where she had no duties. Breuer's intensive therapy helped relieve her of some symptoms, but others replaced them, and when he stopped her treatment, after two years, she was no better than when she began. Many more years were to pass before she could stand on her own.

As with refusals to construct factual memories, the fugue cases and the hysteria of Anna O. indicate that emotional memory failures need not have objective causes. The brain may be in working order, but a person prefers not to remember. Memory focuses intensively on the world as it is, but often that world is not what we would like it to be. These problems seem beyond a doctor's solution. Breuer could listen and help abolish particular hysterical symptoms. Louise's doctor could encourage her growing discontent with "Jeanne's" popularity. But Breuer could do nothing directly about the plight of middle-class women in Viennese society, and Louise's doctor could not repair his patient's isolation and family snarl. Both Anna and Louise saved themselves, and perhaps it could be no other way. To sustain memory people must find something in themselves or in the world that strikes them as worth remembering.

15

FORGETTING
AND OLD AGE

I'm facing the big one, Sidney. Number four-oh. In two
freaking weeks I'll be *middle-aged!* . . . I can't get my
head off my fortieth. I'm taking it real hard. Thank God
for this vacation, take my mind off middle age. First thing
goes is your memory.

—Joseph Wambaugh,
The Secrets of Harry Bright, 1985

Even when we stay eager to live and ready to learn,
time passes. We grow old. Many fatalists hold that senility is
inevitable if you live long enough. Shakespeare's soliloquy about
the seven ages of man agrees. The melancholy Jacques describes
a cycle in which morning-faced schoolchildren ultimately return
to a second childishness where foolish thoughts accompany a
ruined body toward oblivion. Modern folklore continues to
preach that memory's ruin is inevitable by the time a person
reaches seventy or eighty. We have had to add the "or eighty"
clause because the country has plenty of keen-witted seventy-
year-olds. The exceptions that "prove" the rule have grown so
much in evidence that they have modified the rule. Soon the
notion of inevitable senility is likely to seem as absurd as the
learned proofs that women cannot think scientifically.

Somewhere between Shakespeare's day and our own, this
prejudice against the old took on a scientific-sounding justifica-
tion: Neurons in the brain die and are not replaced; by the time

a person reaches seventy (or eighty) so many neurons have died that the mind is bound to fail. This notion ignores how many cells the brain has. Even over a seventy-year period, the random daily destruction of cells simply could not do the damage people credit. We have so many cells that even at a loss rate of one million per day we would have lost only a few percent by age seventy.

Serious memory problems arising from cell death usually follow a stroke. These can kill a large group of cells in a concentrated area and break a memory circuit. The effects of stroke are random and much depends on where the stroke occurs. Sometimes a stroke damages an area but the brain quickly recovers because the corresponding circuit in the other hemisphere continues to function. In other cases the circuits in the two hemispheres do not appear to have developed equally— we are not sure why—and damage is serious and lasting. Many agnosias and aphasias are caused by stroke. The other terrible destroyer of memory is dementia. This disease is less a killer of neurons than a tangler and confuser of them. It snarls and blocks the memory circuit without killing it outright.

Dementia is an uncommon disease, but it brings a devastating loss of previous mental abilities. It is not limited to the elderly, although true to their prejudices against the elderly, doctors called the disease pre-senile dementia when younger people contracted it, and assumed it had a different cause than the senile dementia of the elderly. Only recently have doctors discovered that the two are the same thing. Alzheimer's disease, as the condition has come to be called, is the most common form of dementia. It appears to destroy those areas of the brain, particularly the hippocampus, that control levels above emotional memory, damaging factual memory directly and thereby undermining interpretive memory. But diagnosing Alzheimer's disease is still uncertain and not every elderly person with memory difficulties suffers from it. A survey of recent scholarly articles about Alzheimer's disease shows that a high proportion report new tests and techniques to aid in diagnosis. Although such abundance may sound good, in medicine it usually means that no single test or set of tests is truly satisfactory. When one is found, it will become standard. At present, positive diagnosis requires an examination of the brain after death. Doctors can easily confuse overmedication and more specific functional disorders with Alzheimer's disease. As terrifying as Alzheimer's disease is, it is still rare, seriously affecting only a few percent of the population. For the majority, the news about memory and aging is good! If you stay interested, you stay interesting.

Is Senility Inevitable?

In recent years, memory studies have taken a new look at memory among the elderly. With America's large population of healthy seventy-year-olds and older, it has become increasingly apparent that although some people do suffer catastrophic memory losses, many others do not. Science has begun to ask whether the entire notion of senility could be a myth.

One elaborate memory experiment with the elderly tried to teach them the artificial memory of the ancients. Surprisingly, the subjects found the method easy to learn. Their age became a help because they already had plenty of long experiences with places and they did not have to spend time learning spaces, whereas in the ancient world, young students of rhetoric had to concentrate hard just to learn the places they wished to "walk through." Less surprisingly, it was not clear what benefit artificial memory has to offer the elderly. They too have access to paper and can jot down shopping lists and other things that artificial memory once organized. Even after the lessons, the elderly did not spontaneously add artificial memory techniques to their repertoire. The experiment did yield two lasting lessons, however. It demonstrated that the elderly can still use their memories in disciplined, precise ways. It also proved that you can teach old dogs new tricks. The difficulty in teaching novelties to the elderly lies in persuading them to make the effort.

When learning something seems important, as with improving memory, they catch on quickly.

Success at teaching the old to learn new skills raises questions about an especially widespread belief about the memory of the elderly. The old, we hear, have good memories for the long ago, but poor memories for recent events. Careful study, however, has found that, except among the significantly depressed, the elderly show no measurable difference between the memory for the recent and long past. I have to say "careful study" because sloppy studies do report differences. If you ask old people where they were when they heard about the attack on Pearl Harbor, they can tell you. If you ask what they had for lunch last Tuesday, they do not remember. The obvious difference lies in the level of interest.

This finding is bound to surprise many people. It denies one of the most wide-spread beliefs about the memory of the elderly. When speaking about the memory of the elderly, many people distinguish between "long-term" and "short-term" memories. This commonplace distinction, however, is a creation of the storage metaphor, referring as it does to long- and short-term storage. Because we have found that nothing is stored, we should not be surprised to discover that the long- and short-term distinction does not hold up in careful studies. Memories for recent and for long-ago events depend on the same constructive abilities and the same emotional, factual, and interpretive levels of memory. If a person can still remember past events well and still tell interesting stories about the long ago, he has the equipment to do the same for more recent events. Failure to remember the present in such cases suggests a failure to pay attention to the present, not an inability to learn new details.

Reduced interest does not imply a lost capacity for attention. The two forms of attention that carry a person of any age to the factual memory level are prompt recall and the orientation reaction. Prompt recall appears to show no lessening with age, and the orientation reaction persists as well. I have seen very old people literally on their death bed come to attention when an unexpected friend came through the door. A general disappearance or weakening of the orientation reaction in a person of any age probably indicates depression. Factual and interpretive memory depend on attention, which in turn requires a healthy interest and curiosity. Depression severely reduces a person's attention to the environment and harms memory even though the brain has no organic problems.

Depression accounts for many of the familiar problems among the aged. One study questioned the families and elderly outpatients at a psychiatric clinic about the patients' memories. Patients also had their memories tested. To the surprise of the researchers, tests showed that by objective standards patients who complained of failing memory had no worse memories than those patients who were not troubled by memory problems. Patients worried about their memories, however, tended to be significantly more depressed. These findings can mean two things. The depression could imply that memory is fine, but the person is so down on himself that he just assumes a serious problem lies behind any evidence of faltering memory. It could also be that depression actively interferes with memory. Both factors are probably at work.

I have seen the effects of depression on my own memory. For many years I have played a mental game with myself. I pick a bygone date at random and try to remember a conversation I had on that date. Usually I can remember something that I heard said around that time, but through this game I have discovered two black holes in my life, periods in which I draw a blank and remember little or nothing. Both of those times were periods of depression over the way my life was going. Those were young times in my life and I did not even realize that my memory was not up to par, but if I had been elderly I might well have been more alert to the notion of memory difficulties and interpreted them as proof of my declining mental powers. No doubt such a conclusion would have deepened my depression. The deepened depression would have slowed my memory even more. I would have become still more depressed. This dreadful cycle can sustain itself endlessly.

The End of Fatalism

Laboratory testing has turned up one important difference between the memory of youth and that of old age. Experiments with list learning showed that recall powers decline over the whole age range, but recognition powers remain stable. These experiments used meaningless lists and suggest that over a lifetime memory's balance shifts in favor of meaning. In youth, the world is unknown and confusing. We need to learn how the world is and then try to make sense of it. As we grow older, we know more about how the world works and need to know how something fits in with past experience. Recognition, therefore, does not fade. Its stability supports the one favorable stereotype about the elderly—they have seen much and know the implications of events.

Research has not destroyed all the old notions about memory and aging nor declared them to be purest nonsense. It does, however, deny the fatalism that accompanied the notions. Many of the things known about normal memory do have implications for old age:

- Absentmindedness results from automatic or routine behavior, from not paying attention. If a life is largely dull routine, many of its details are forgotten the instant they occur. This principle holds true at any age, but may be especially true for those older people who seldom do anything out of the ordinary.

- Factual memory stays generalized unless a person pays attention to aspects of context that make a particular incident unusual. Children and young people who have yet to encounter many ordinary things meet a continuing series of "firsts" to remember, but an older person finds much less under the sun that seems new.

- Interpretive memory develops from insight to insight, and insight depends on wrestling with experience, discovering its depth. As a person grows older, many problems seem solved, and it is easy to stay with insights formed decades ago. In more traditional societies, the slow steady accrual of insight gives old people strong grounds for respect, but in our rapidly changing world some unrevised insights will become out of date.

• All memory depends on active movement up through its levels, and action demands physical energy. As people grow older and have less energy, moving up the staircase may become more and more like climbing a real flight of stairs. They can do it, but it takes longer and the temptation to stop at a lower level grows more enticing.

In each of these cases we see similar themes. Memory depends on staying interested, staying alert, and staying active. People have not just dreamed up the memory problems of old age, but they have been cruelly fatalistic in supposing that any difficulties signify an irreversible decline in mental powers.

PART
FOUR

THE EXPERIENCE
OF MEMORY

16

MEMORY AND LIFE

In psychological analysis we must never forget the utili-
tarian character of our mental functions, which are essentially turned towards action.

—Henri Bergson, *Matter and Memory*, 1911

Constructing and climbing a memory staircase is not an unambiguous mark of progress. Much of our adaptive power comes from using the interpretive level of memory, but much of our humanity and vitality is already visible at memory's emotional level. The construction of a new step on a staircase has a price. The time I began to remember Swahili vocabulary after one hearing of a word offers an example of the losses that accompany a gain. Of course my speaking fluency began to accelerate, but my wonder at the language's music faded. During the first month of lessons, this new language sounded magical and marvelous. After I began to recognize the sounds in a word my amazement disappeared and never returned. By now it has been so long that I have no sense at all of the foreignness of the language and its words. In particular there had been that special word of greeting that pleased me, and after adding a new step on my Swahili stairs I could remember the word whenever I wanted it. Unfortunately, however, the word no longer seemed as wondrous. It was just a word with a particular use and meaning. I had once thought that if only I could remember the word I should love to say it, but when I could remember it easily the fun of saying it seemed less satisfying.

Because of the practical benefits in learning the language and because I wanted to learn it, I have no doubt that in this instance the gains in my memory outweighed the costs; however, sometimes the price can seem too high. Many forms of work that seem nightmarish and dehumanizing use only higher levels of memory and ignore the lower ones. A keyboard operator, for example, may pass the day putting the information on handwritten forms into a computer. Such work is still done by people because computers cannot yet read handwriting with anything close to the accuracy necessary to do the job. People use interpretive-level recognition to perceive handwriting, and interpretive-level recall to type what they recognize. Postal workers, many office typists, and check handlers at banks spend all day concentrating on this work. Although it depends on interpretive memory skills enjoyed only by humans, the work satisfies no desires and deepens no curiosity. It is precisely the absence of a role for memory's lower levels that makes such work seem dehumanizing. We cannot assume, therefore, that the upper levels of memory are superior to the lower.

In this final section of the book we will consider three individuals and see how their memories worked and served them. These three cases differ from the examples found in ''The Forgettery'' because they have no pathology. The people differ according to what we can call their styles of remembering, but we do not know of any organic or neurotic problem that prevented them from using all of their memories. Their styles depend on all of the principles that have emerged from our study of memory: Memory is a construction of the imagination; it is produced as much by subjective factors as by objective ones; and it serves to adapt behavior to present circumstances. Consequently, when appraising and describing an individual's memory, we can no longer content ourselves with attempts to measure a memory's storage capacity or to score a memory's accuracy nor with any set of purely objective standards.

Traditional attempts to evaluate memory usually begin with tests, variations on Ebbinghaus's experimental techniques with lists, that try to measure a person's storage space and the rate at which he can shovel in new data. They allow an examiner to report that a person's memory is average, above average, or below average. Unfortunately, these results have almost no predictive value concerning the quality of a person's behavior. Instead of relying on the fallacious notion of storage, the chapters in this section consider the level of memory a person finds satisfactory to his understanding of an experience. Any appraisal of a person's memory must include a consideration of the levels he uses in remembering.

We do not have to climb to the top of a memory staircase every time we act, not even to act well. With some things we can hesitate to climb at all. For example, even very young children can enjoy dancing spontaneously to music. Other creatures do not act that way, but for reasons both mysterious and joyful, our species does. A two-year-old I knew with precocious language skills once told me, "Music makes me happy," and as she spoke she improvised a dance. Her memory levels were not terribly high; her action seemed almost a motor association, like riding a bicycle, yet her action and memory suited the occasion. Grown people too may feel content to bring no more than this level with them when going dancing. They have a good time at a dance and ask no more from their outing. Others, of course, do observe as well as enjoy. Besides dancing, they pay attention to how guests are dressed and they will remember who came with whom. A minority may also interpret what they see, understanding the relationships they see around them. They know which dancers' hearts have been broken, and who is moving toward seduction. At the end of the evening these different people have different memories of the party because they care to know different things:—*"It was fun."*—*"That Priscilla Dumont looked so beautiful in pink."*—*"I believe Scarlett likes Captain Butler more than she admits."* But although they remember different things and use different memory levels, no one can say whose memory is best. It is a case of to each his own, and there is no basis for making a final judgment.

Traditional accounts of memory have always tried to appraise and explain memory through purely objective causes. Behaviorists sought the cause in objective stimuli outside a person. Newer schools of psychology looked both to stimuli and to memories stored in the head. But we now find that the construction of memory includes subjective causes like desire, continuing attention, and interpretation. Emotions and ambitions have much to do with the memory level a person prefers to use. There may be no objective reason that one person remembers a ball on the emotional level whereas a friend remembers it on the factual level. Their brains may be similarly endowed and their circumstances at the party might match, but their desires differ. The party-goer whose style favors emotional memory may, the next day, have a sense that there was a new type of music that is enjoyable to dance to. The friend whose style leans to factual memory may recall that a new color is gaining favor with the fashion leaders. Thus, a discussion of memory has to explore motivation as well as memory levels. Of course, even though different interests lead people to remember different things, it would be absurd to say one desire is superior to the other because it takes a higher level of memory to satisfy it.

Memory's adaptive role offers a basis for judging quality. Memory must answer the question of what to do now, and some solutions do work better than others. Adaptation always implies adapting to something for some reason, and it provides a context for judging a memory despite its subjective motivation. Biologists have long considered contextual matters, and they know that objective measures are the least informative approach to a subject. A biological study of birds' wings, for example, could develop a gross ranking from longest to shortest, but understanding comes only through a consideration of a bird's flying needs and accomplishments. That issue quickly leads a biologist away from objective measures and into questions about aerodynamics and about the bird's habitat.

A biologist considering an animal's memory abilities must also ask about the context and habitat. If a biologist compared the memories of a gazelle and a lion, he would soon notice that the lion sometimes seems to climb fairly well up a memory staircase. Lions can concentrate during a hunt and adapt their behavior to the swiftly changing situation. Gazelles operate much lower on a staircase. Their greatest feat may be just recognizing lions when they see them, but the gazelle has no need for memory's upper levels. It eats grass and the grass does not run away. Neither does the gazelle have to outwit the charging lion, only outrun it. No biologist would care to argue that the lion's memory is *better* than the gazelle's. Each has a memory suited to its circumstances.

At the same time, the limitations on an animals' memory do put boundaries on its use of a habitat. George Schaller, an American biologist who spent years observing lions in the wild, reports that both leopards and lions are in competition for gazelles. Leopards like to haul their gazelle carcasses up into trees and feed on them at a leisurely rate over several days. Lions prefer to eat their gazelles at one sitting, and if they could get at the hanging carcasses, their thieving would become a major annoyance to leopards. Lions are not the great tree climbers that leopards are, but they do climb and could get at many of the gazelle carcasses. Yet memory limitations make it almost unknown for a lion to steal the leopard's cache. After a day or two under the African sun a gazelle carcass is ripe enough to draw lions to the trees the way the smell of strawberries draws children. The lions circle and stare up into the branches. They look straight at the dangling carcass, but the meat is twisted in a peculiar way and is in a bizarre context. The lions look and smell, but Schaller says, they cannot recognize the thing above their heads. This limit on their imagination sets a bound to their ability to exploit their environment just as surely as the physical limitations on their strength and speed circumscribe their capacities.

In the three chapters that follow, we shall try to see the relation between memory and life. The individuals had memory styles quite different from one another, but they also had distinctive purposes and tastes that change the context of our evaluation. In each case an appraisal depends on how well a person's memory adapted him to the pursuit of his own desires.

17

THE EMOTIONAL
MEMORY OF
JOHN DEAN

I would say I have an ability to recall, not specific words
necessarily, but certainly the tenor of a conversation and
the gist of a conversation. . . . my mind is not a tape
recorder, but it certainly receives the message that is
being given.

—John Dean, *Senate testimony*, 1973

In the summer of 1973, John Dean appeared before
televised hearings about the Watergate scandal. He was one of
the most devastating witnesses any tribunal had ever seen. He
spoke coolly and dispassionately, describing an easily understood, coherent story of justice obstructed. Other Watergate
witnesses tended to retreat quickly into pleas that memory failed
them. They would not deny that something had happened, but
would say they could not recollect what had really transpired.
This convenient forgetfulness frustrated and raised suspicions in
observers, but John Dean boasted of his wonderful memory and
many people took him at his word. Observers called him the
man with the tape-recorder memory and listened in awe as he
reported details of old conversations.

A comparison of Dean's testimony with the facts, however,
indicates that Dean had a terrible memory. Investigators settled

the question of Nixon's guilt long ago, using evidence much more reliable than one man's self-serving memory, so when I report that John Dean's memory was abominable, I do not mean there was no Watergate conspiracy. I mean simply that Dean's memory was awful, awful in both the ordinary sense that Dean got his facts wrong and in the sense that Dean's memory led his judgment desperately astray.

At the time of Dean's testimony, it seemed as though his memory's accuracy would always be subject to partisan dispute, but then the world learned that Nixon had secretly tape recorded meetings in the Oval Office and it became possible to test Dean's memory directly. Memory students suddenly had a natural experiment permitting them to compare one man's recollection with what really happened.

Dean's testimony and the related transcripts are too long for a full analysis, but we can consider one incident in detail. Dean described a meeting he had on September 15, 1972, with Richard Nixon and Nixon's chief of staff, Robert Haldeman. The meeting's purpose was to discuss the indictment of the Watergate burglars and some of their bosses. From the White House's perspective, the indictments had brought good news because nobody had been charged whose name had not previously appeared in the press. Particularly, the indictments did not expose the role of top officers of the Nixon campaign committee in financing and organizing the burglary. Most of the conversation at the White House meeting, however, was not about the indictments, but about the revenge the administration would take on the people who had made the Watergate incident so uncomfortable for the president.

To examine Dean's memory we can compare his testimony with the transcript. The left-hand column below presents Dean's entire statement about his meeting with the president, broken up claim by claim. The right-hand column presents relevant excerpts from the transcript of the tape recordings of the meeting. These excerpts do not appear in their proper sequence, that of the transcript, because Dean did not always remember things in their order of occurrence.

DEAN'S TESTIMONY	TRANSCRIPT
The President told me that Bob [Haldeman] had kept him posted on my handling of the Watergate case,	
told me I had done a good job	PRES: The way you have handled all this seems to me has been very skillful, putting your fingers in the leaks that have sprung here and sprung there.
and he appreciated how difficult a task it had been	
and the President was pleased that the case had stopped with Liddy.	
I told him that I thought there was a long way to go before this matter would end	DEAN: Three months ago I would have had trouble predicting there would be a day when this would be forgotten, but I think I can say that 54 days from now [election day] nothing is going to come crashing down to our surprise.
and I certainly could make no assurances that the day would not come when the matter would start to unravel.	
Early in our conversation the President said to me that former FBI Director Hoover had told him shortly after he had assumed office in 1969	
that his campaign had been bugged in 1968.	PRES: We were bugged in '68 on the plane . . . the FBI did the bugging.
The President said that at some point we should get the facts out on this	DEAN: It is a shame that evidence to the fact that that happened in '68 was never around . . .
and use this to counter the problems that we were encountering.	PRES: It isn't worth it—the hell with it.

The President asked me when the criminal case would come to trial and would it start before the election.

I told the President that I did not know.

I said that the Justice Department had held off as long as possible the return of the indictments,

but much would depend on which judge got the case.

The President said that he certainly hoped that the case would not come to trial before the election.

The conversation then moved to the press coverage of the Watergate incident and how the press was really trying to make this into a major campaign issue.

At one point in this conversation I recall the President telling me to keep a good list of the press people giving us trouble

because we will make life difficult for them after the election.

The conversation then turned to the use of the Internal Revenue Service to attack our enemies.

I recall telling the President that we had not made much use of this because the White House did not have the clout to have it done,

DEAN: One of the things I've tried to do, I have begun to keep notes on a lot of people who are emerging as less than our friends . . .
PRES: I want the most comprehensive notes on all those who tried to do us in . . . It has to be done.
DEAN: . . . this will be over some day and we shouldn't forget the way some of them have treated us.

PRES: . . . We have not used the Bureau [of Internal Revenue] and we have not used the Justice Department but things are going to change now. And they are either going to do it right or go.
DEAN: What an exciting prospect.

that the Internal Revenue Service
was a rather Democratically
oriented bureaucracy

and it would be very dangerous to
try any such activities.

The President seemed somewhat
annoyed

and said that the Democratic
administrations had used this tool
well

and after the election we would get
people in these agencies who would
be responsive to the White House
requirements.

If the reader is like me and remembers accepting as gospel every word Dean spoke, this comparison may be something of a shock. Dean's memory was terrible. Of the twenty-six separate assertions in Dean's testimony, fourteen have no historical basis, seven are badly distorted, and two are completely false. That leaves three correct assertions—the assertion that the Nixon campaign was bugged in '68 and the part about the president's praise and his appreciation of Dean's skill. Even in the latter memory we have an inaccuracy; the president's praise came much later in the meeting than Dean said.

It took my breath away to compile this side-by-side comparison and then read the senators' questions about this testimony. In one exchange Senator Howard Baker questioned Dean closely about several events that never happened.

BAKER: . . . can you give us any further insight into what the president said?

DEAN: Yes, I can recall he told me that he appreciated how difficult a job it had been for me.

BAKER: Is that close to the exact language?

DEAN: Yes, that is close to the exact language. That stuck very clearly in my mind because I recall my response to that was that I didn't feel that I could take credit. I thought that others had done much more difficult things and by that I was referring to the fact that Mr. Magruder had perjured himself.

BAKER: All right. Now, tell us about the status of the case.

DEAN: When we talked about the fact that the indictments had been handed down, at some point, and after the compliment I told him at that point that we had managed, you know, that the matter had been contained, it had not come in to the White House. I didn't say that, I said it had been contained.

BAKER: What was the president's or Mr. Haldeman's reaction to that word because that is a rather significant word, I think.

DEAN: Everyone seemed to understand what I was talking about. It didn't evoke any questions and I was going on to say that I didn't think it could be contained indefinitely. I said that is this, you know, there are a lot of hurdles that have to be leaped down the road before it will definitely remain contained and I was trying to tell the president that I was not sure the cover-up even then would last indefinitely.

BAKER: What was his reaction to this?

DEAN: As I say, I don't recall any particular reaction.

BAKER: Was there any statement by him or by Mr. Haldeman at that point on this statement?

DEAN: No, not to my recollection.

No wonder Dean's recollection on the details is so vague. With one exception, none of the things Dean testifies to in this passage occurred. The president's appreciation for how hard the work had been, Dean's refusal to take credit, Dean's use of the word *contained,* Dean's warning of further hurdles down the road— these never happened. The one thing that Dean says never happened did happen. Dean said he never talked about keeping the investigation out of the White House. The transcript shows, however, that Haldeman did say the indictments had been "kept away from the White House and of course the president,'' and Dean piped in to agree. Dean's one accurate memory is that the president praised him. Dean keeps returning to this point, and Nixon did briefly praise his work.

A study of the transcript shows that besides remembering things that never happened Dean forgot many things that would have helped his case. Nixon did promise revenge for all the problems Watergate had brought. "Just remember all the trouble we're taking," he told Dean. "We'll have a chance to get back one day." He did describe precisely the purposes of the cover-up, telling Dean, "You just try to button it up as well as you can and hope for the best, and remember basically the damn business is unfortunately trying to cut our losses." If Dean had quoted this remark in his testimony, it would have caused an uproar, but he said nothing.

At one point during the meeting Nixon specifically brought his authority into the cover-up, saying, "This is a big play. He [Dick Cook, the White House's assistant liaison with Congress] has to know that it comes from the top. While I can't talk for myself, he has to get at this and——the thing up." So Dean did not have to make up evidence indicating the president's role in the conspiracy.

Dean also omitted a whole raft of thuggish ideas that were discussed—a fantasy about tormenting Edward Bennett Williams (a prominent Democrat), strategies for hitting enemies with civil suits, a judge who whispers helpful things to them, ways to threaten majority leader Tip O'Neill. These too would have helped Dean's case, but he left them out.

At the time of the hearings people asked if Dean's testimony was true or false. Was he a liar? Was his memory accurate? But these questions are too crude to get at the reality of Dean's testimony, which had managed to use a wealth of phony details to describe a real conspiracy. This paradox of truth based on misinformation points at one of the crucial differences between the old and new way of thinking about memory. The old idea assumed that memory was a store of objective information about the past. Points of view, generalized descriptions, and the nature of the circumstances all arose from the facts. Those assumptions made it impossible to suggest that a witness under oath could have misremembered the facts and still have testified to something true.

The paradox of Dean's testimony challenges us to find a new way to discuss his memory. The first memory scholar to try to describe and understand Dean's testimony was Ulric Neisser, a founding father of cognitive psychology. In 1981 he published an article about Dean's memory in the scholarly journal *Cognition*. Neisser was horrified by the paradoxical tangle. He found that even techniques for measuring the "gist" of a conversation showed Dean's memory was almost always awful, unless Dean reported a conversation that he had actively prepared for. But at the same time Dean did not invent the whole situation. There had been a cover-up; he had participated in it, and Richard Nixon had put himself at the head of it. Neisser said that Dean told a "higher truth." Let me suggest an alternate phrase. Dean told a "lower truth." Generalizations lie at the lower levels of memory's steps; the details come higher up. A person who hears forty binary digits and says, "I heard a bunch of numbers," is not wrong, not lying, but his memory has not climbed as high as the person who can recite those forty digits. Dean's memory was not the sort that produced episodic chunks of conversation, but he did not invent his basic premise.

In some respects Dean's memory reminds one of an amnesiac who tends to confabulate the details of his story. The supposed facts are plausible and the very energy behind their assertion gives them a certain credibility, but they are fantasies. One important difference, however, was the coherence in Dean's story. An amnesiac's confabulation tends to come apart like a dream whereas Dean's story hung together. Remarkably, however, Dean testified that the coherence of his story did not come from his own memory for the logic that underlay events. In response to questioning from Hawaii's Senator Daniel Inouye Dean said he took the basic structure of his story from the press. He testified:

> What I did in preparing this statement, I had kept a newspaper clipping file from roughly June 17 [date of the Watergate arrests] up until about the time these hearings started when I stopped doing any clipping with any regularity. It was by going through every single newspaper article outlining what had happened and then placing myself in what I had done in a given sequence of time, I was aware of all of the principal activities I had been involved in, the dealings I had had with others in relationship to these activities.

His system used the newspaper clips as reminders. That system can work, but there is no guarantee that the reminders will produce accurate recall of the past instead of confabulations. It does guarantee, however, that one's testimony will not contradict the public record, and one of the strength's of Dean's testimony was the way it dovetailed with the known facts about Watergate.

Although this method gave Dean's testimony a coherent structure, his details were not always logical. After pressing Dean to account for his memory, Senator Inouye questioned him on a logical contradiction in the testimony. Dean had said that at his September 15 meeting the president was fully aware of the cover-up and Dean's role in it. A study of the transcript confirms this general claim; however, in his opening statement Dean also described his second meeting with the president, one that occurred over four months later, at the end of February 1973. According to Dean's testimony, at this meeting he informed the president of his own role in the cover-up, but the president denied that Dean had legal problems:

> Before departing his office, [the president] again raised the matter that I should report to him directly and not through Haldeman and Ehrlichman. I told him that I thought he should know that I was also involved in the post-June 17 activities regarding Watergate. I briefly described to him why I thought I had legal problems, in that I had been a conduit for many of the decisions that were made and therefore could be involved in an obstruction of justice. He would not accept my analysis

and did not want me to get into it in any detail other than what I had just related. He reassured me not to worry, that I had no legal problems.

Senator Inouye repeatedly asked why Dean had thought it necessary in February to explain his role to the president if Mr. Nixon had been fully aware of that role the previous September. Dean had no clear explanation for this inconsistency, and how could he since what he described never happened? It might be interesting to speculate on how the course of history could have changed if the senator had chosen to press the issue. Instead, Senator Inouye dropped the matter and it did not return.

The transcripts show that the contradiction arose because Dean's memory for the February meeting was no better than his memory for the September one. The business about telling Dean to bypass Haldeman and Ehrlichman did not happen. Dean's reference to his own problems arose in a different context altogether:

PRESIDENT: There is no question what [the people on the Senate select committee] are after. What the Committee is after is somebody at the White House. They would like to get Haldeman, or Colson, or Ehrlichman.

DEAN: Or possibly Dean—You know, I am a small fish.

PRES: Anybody in the White House they would—but in your case I think they realize you are the lawyer and they know you didn't have a (adjective deleted) to do with the campaign.

DEAN: That's right.

PRES: That's what I think. Well, we'll see you.

Dean's self-pitying characterization of himself as a small fish hardly matches his testimony about describing his role as a conduit for decisions. The exchange was not an effort to make the president fully aware of things he had not appreciated before. Instead, it reads like the remarks of a man who has suddenly become nervous about his own vulnerability.

While Senator Inouye briefly challenged the internal consistency of Dean's story, Senator Edward Gurney of Florida challenged an aspect of the public record that had not appeared in the newspapers:

GURNEY: I would like to go back to the Kalmbach meeting again, when you and he first discussed this cover-up money.

DEAN: On the 29th, Senator? He was staying at the Mayflower Hotel . . .

GURNEY: Well, the committee has subpoenaed the records of the hotel. I have a letter here from the Mayflower, and also from the Statler Hilton. The letter is from the Mayflower Hotel, "Dear Senator Gurney, the records do not reflect a Mr. Herbert B. Kalmbach, as being a registered guest during the period June 1, 1972, through July 1, 1972." Then the other letter from the Statler Hilton, again addressed to me, "Mr. Herbert W. Kalmbach was registered in our hotel from June 29–30, 1972." Now, you have testified three times that you met with Mr. Kalmbach in the coffee shop of the Mayflower Hotel . . .

DEAN: I see what you are saying. I have testified the Mayflower and I am never sure which is the Mayflower and which the Statler Hilton.

GURNEY: Well, I must say I am reminded of your colloquy with the chairman yesterday, Mr. Dean, when you said what an excellent memory you had right from school days.

At this point Dean's lawyer whispered something that reporter John Chancellor had just revealed to the television audience, and Dean said, "I might go back over one point. The name of the coffee shop at the Statler Hilton is the Mayflower." The audience burst into applause, tipping its sentiments. Everybody could understand the confusion between Mayflower Coffee Shop and Mayflower Hotel.

Senator Gurney saw his fish get away. Given the either/or discussions of truth and memory, the cross-examination had failed. The old lawyer's tool of discrediting important memories by challenging a trivial one did not work. Instead it bolstered Dean's reputation. But Senator Gurney had hit on a telling example of the difficulties in Dean's memory. The confusion of Mayflower Coffee Shop for Mayflower Hotel is a typical recall error in psychological laboratory experiments, yet Dean was not participating in an experiment. He had not only the name, but the experience of the meeting to refer to. Normally, in laboratory experiments, when a memory becomes this much richer, confusions over meaningless similarities disappear. Dean's statement was not casually written. He had worked on it for weeks or perhaps months. Our study of interpretive memory leads us to expect a conflict in a normal person: The name Mayflower clashes with the remembered images of the incident. We should expect a bothered John Dean preparing his statement to say, "Something is wrong. I keep thinking Mayflower, but it doesn't feel right." Apparently, Dean was not bothered, or at least not bothered enough to get that detail right. He seems content not to press his memory.

In appraising John Dean's memory we must carefully distinguish between memory's levels. Interpretive memory normally provides the structure that organizes what we recall, but Dean took his structure from the newspapers. Interpretive memory also uses the tension between recall and recognition to get the details straight. Dean seems not to have had a bothered memory either. His testimony offers no good evidence that he ever benefited from memory's top level in preparing his testimony.

Factual memory uses reminders to recall associations. Dean's newspaper technique relied entirely on reminders, but we have seen that often he remembered things that never happened. In some cases factual associations were probably stirred—as in his recall of a discussion about the bugging of Nixon's 1968 campaign—but the associations became grossly distorted when placed in narrative form. At this middle level, Dean's memory was still too unreliable to justify faith in anything he proclaimed as a fact.

On the emotional level, however, Dean's memory suddenly became a good one. At this level a perception evokes an emotion, and Dean's memory for the emotions of his meetings with the president were good. The newspaper technique did not remind him of trustworthy facts, but the emotions they evoked were to the point. Emotionally, the September 15 meeting had brought praise from the president. Dean remembered that pleasure. The implications of the praise—that Nixon understood and approved of Dean's behavior—were also correct.

The February meeting that so troubled Senator Inouye had a very different emotional association. By then the Watergate affair was destroying people who had seemed beyond harm's way, and Dean expressed anxiety about his own skin. Dean was correct that the president was not "fully aware" of the situation as it applied to Dean, if by those words Dean meant that the president did not yet appreciate the danger to Dean. The president was not as worried about Dean's skin as Dean was. Again, Dean was correct in his emotional association.

We must be careful. John Dean's memory has not been evaluated and tested by professionals. We cannot be conclusive. We can only look for suggestive patterns that might help articulate the workings of his memory. To me, it appears that John Dean was largely content to settle for the work of emotional memory. It seems that he could use other memory levels but often preferred not to. In Part Three we saw that people who, for pathological reasons, cannot advance beyond emotional memory suffer from amnesia. John Dean was not a true amnesiac. He did not suffer from their disorientation and there is no evidence or even any suggestion that he had any brain damage. Yet his memory for the details of events does come close to confabulation.

The difference between amnesia and a reliance on emotional memory is the difference between ability and desire. An amnesiac cannot recall something, no matter how desperately he might want to and no matter how alert he was at the time of the original experience. John Dean, however, seems simply to have been uninterested in the world beyond himself. Like all normal people, his memory began with the question of what something meant to himself. But it also stopped there. The curiosity and insight that send some people higher up the stairs appears not to have moved him.

Dean's Watergate memoirs are full of passages that support the view of a man content to live on memory's emotional level. One example of Dean's distaste for the factual level comes from his account of the early morning staff meetings at the White House. The right to attend these sessions was a mark of status, and Dean wangled that right. At the briefings the cabinet and departmental leaders reported on their work in progress. It was a singular opportunity for an ambitious young lawyer to learn how the republic really works, but Dean found the meetings boring. They had nothing to do with his direct responsibilities, and after a while he quit attending them. Like someone habituating to a list of names, Dean switched his attention elsewhere. It was a definite refusal to enrich his factual memory.

Dean's memoirs also tell a story of his preference for staying on memory's emotional level. When Dean was first offered a job in the White House, the president was staying at his home in San Clemente, California. Dean flew out to Los Angeles. There he found a helicopter standing by to fly him on to the "Western White House." The helicopter could have been an appealing symbol of his new prestige; however, Dean had ridden in government helicopters several times before and those times had not been prestigious. Dean says, "I preferred not to think about those previous trips because now I was relishing the glamour." We have seen that associations enrich factual memory, but Dean wanted to keep his associations at bay because they undercut the supposed glamor of the White House. Here we see John Dean, "the man with the tape-recorder mind," refusing to use memory because it disrupts his fantasies.

One might wonder how Dean ever accomplished anything if, given his druthers, he preferred to stay on memory's emotional level. His memoirs provide an amazing answer. Like a bored worker on an assembly line, he was motivated to produce by a force that came entirely from outside himself. To make sure people did their work, chief of staff Haldeman used a technique known as "tickling," keeping pressure on a person to perform. A tickler was a person who made sure that assignments were done on time. The tickler would telephone and demand results. A staffer might dillydally; the tickler would accept no excuses. Dean describes this tickler system as a kind of inhuman machine:

> The discipline of Haldeman's tickler was unrelenting. . . . I had answered [my first assignment] on time, but subsequently I spent too much time preparing my answers to a few action memoranda, let the due dates slide by, and discovered the consequences. . . . The tickler was . . . probably more responsible for the chief of staff's awesome reputation than was his own aluminum personality. It was a self-perpetuating paper monster, with a computer's memory and a Portuguese man-of-war's touch. . . . Once a staff man was nailed with responsibility for the slightest project, the tickler would keep pestering until it was fed something. . . . No one could ignore the tickler.

So there was the White House system. It exerted unrelenting pressure to produce. The pressure to act came not from Dean's soul or from his interest in the project, but from the imposition of fear. Dean was not moved to learn more, but to ease the pressure he felt. Presumably, the reports he wrote reflected factual and interpretive memory for the law, but the motive for reaching those levels came from outside himself.

Dean's memoirs report that he had long preferred to suppress any arousal he felt. The tendency helped him during his Senate testimony since Dean's greatest strength as a witness surely was the cool dispassion with which he spoke. Few observers would have called him "emotional," but of course emotional memory does not mean passionate or excited memory. It means memory that focuses solely on immediate circumstances and personal feeling. Factual associations and interpretive perceptions have nothing to contribute to this level of memory. Arousal helps factual memory, and observers almost universally noticed Dean's absence of arousal.

Dean's coldness helped make him seem credible, but if he really did depend too heavily on emotional memory, this lack of arousal is probably what tripped him up. Dean's own memoirs provide some insight into his weakened orientation response. He describes the first feeler he received from the White House about a job, and says of his response, "As always, I was masking my inner calculations and feelings, this time behind an appearance of friendly sincerity." We cannot be certain that he behaved this way in that interview, but Dean says *as always,* meaning that he routinely hid his feelings behind a mask. This attitude corresponds to the public's impression of a cold, perpetually collected man who never wore his heart on his sleeve.

Later Dean refers to his visit to Nixon's "Western White House" in San Clemente, and he reports, "I decided I had handled my escalating headiness fairly well. I had been cool, had controlled my excitement, yet had managed a little hustling." Again, the accuracy of this memory is not at issue, but the attitude. Dean felt it was important to bury his excitement. He found he could do it and still function.

Dean speculates briefly about why he routinely suppresses his own arousal and says, "I suspect it is the fear of failure or rejection that sets off this defense mechanism in me before *any* interview." (Emphasis mine.) At last we see a reason for shunning the world: It can be a place of disappointment and rejection. To defend against potential pains, Dean hid his excitement from the world. Some people manage to look calm while drinking in everything; however, Dean adds, "I wanted to make a mental adjustment. I would have to collect my thoughts fast, and I would have to start telling myself I did not even want to work at the White House." So, Dean's routine was to mask his interest both from the world and from himself.

Because Dean preferred not to build memory stairs above the emotional level, it becomes a matter of opinion whether we should fault him for not remembering the facts and organization of the events he testified to. Some people will insist these things should be remembered correctly; others will take a less judgmental stand and say that it all worked out in the end. There is no reason automatically to denigrate emotional memory and its categorization of the world as good-for-me, bad-for-me, and irrelevant-to-me. This focus blinded Dean to many facts but it let him distinguish sharply between his friends and his enemies. He understood that distinction well. One rare time the transcripts show Dean balk at a direct instruction from Nixon concerned the treatment of Cartha DeLoach, deputy director of the FBI. This conversation took place when the cover-up was collapsing. The president wanted to destroy the career of Patrick Gray, acting head of the FBI, and he was not too worried about how it was done, but Dean feared that if done too crudely DeLoach too could be destroyed, and DeLoach was a friend of theirs.

The transcript shows the president's reply to Dean's concern as "(Expletive deleted)."

Dean, however, did not back down, but said he thought DeLoach was a friend.

Nixon replied, "Nobody's a friend of ours. Let's face it. Don't worry about that sort of thing."

And Dean still balked, saying he would explore the matter further with his advisor, Dick Moore.

Conceivably John Dean could have had a satisfactory career in the White House. He could have persisted at identifying and remembering the people who were useful to him. The ticklers could have gone on teasing reports out of him, and he could have continued enjoying the flimsy perks and prestige of office like helicopter rides. But then a crisis developed. Burglars were caught in the Watergate offices of the National Democratic Party. Within a short time the press reported that some of the burglars were linked to employees of Nixon's reelection committee. In the White House there was general consternation. People of judgment grew panicky and tried to dissociate themselves from the event. Dean's memoirs describe frightened staff people trying to hide evidence that could connect them to the episode. But Dean did not panic because, in the words of an old joke, he did not understand the situation. He thought the burglary could hurt others, but not himself. It is as though he feared his own excitement and disappointment, but did not fear distant things in the outside world.

At this point the limitations of emotional memory come sharply into view. It deals with the world only as the senses find it. It does not remind us of associated dangers that may arise, nor does it let us construct likely problems. When Watergate began, Dean reacted as though his big chance to bolster his position within the White House had come, but his memory was too limited for him to adapt to the dangers of the situation.

The bill had come due for all those staircases he had preferred not to construct. He should have known that the White House is not a monarchy and behind its glamor stands the reality of a robust democracy. He should have known too that the White House's power is severely limited by the various interests of the people it deals with. Surely that point was made a thousand times during the morning briefings on White House work in progress, but Dean paid no attention to those meetings. So when confronted with one of the most politically dangerous moments in the history of the White House Dean lacked the equipment to imagine that danger. Instead, he behaved so blindly that at first many people were hard put to believe that the stories of Watergate could be true. Bribing burglars to be silent and suborning perjury while leaving a telltale trail of banking documentation seemed too dumb to have been possible. When it came to answering the fundamental question of what do I do now, John Dean's memory served him worse than ill. It ruined him and the people who had sought to use him.

18

THE FACTUAL

MEMORY

OF S

Mnemonic systems are typically not particularly helpful
in remembering the sort of information which one requires in everyday life. They are, of course, excellent for
learning the strings of unrelated words which are so close
to the hearts of experimental psychologists, but I must
confess that if I need to remember a shopping list, I do
not imagine strings of sausages festooned from my chan-
deliers and bunches of bananas sprouting from my ward-
robe. I simply write it down.

—Alan Baddeley, *The Psychology of Memory*, 1976

In 1968 the Russian neuroscientist Aleksandr Luria
published a fascinating little book about the memory of a man
he identified only as S. (S for Shereshevsky, his family name.)
Tovarisch S was born in Russia just before the turn of the
century and came to Luria's attention when he was already an
adult. At the time of their first meeting S worked as a journalist.
His editor had learned that S never bothered to take notes
because he never forgot anything. Intrigued, the editor sent S to
Luria for testing. Luria proceeded to give the standard memory
span tests—randomized lists of words for recall. To his surprise,

S's memory span did not stop at five, seven, or even fourteen. It was apparently limitless. Time seemed to have no effect on it either. Sixteen years after these tests, Luria surprised S with a request to repeat a list and S did so, perfectly.

Luria himself was one of this century's greatest neuroscientists, some people even say that he was *the* greatest. His importance rested on a keen eye that let him see the many discrepancies between theoretical expectation and actual experience. Here, Luria saw that S contradicted the many assumptions about storage that were favored by the memory theory of his day. Psychologists in the late 1920s assumed that memories were held somewhere in the head and that it took time to assimilate them. Ebbinghaus and his followers thought that memory was seriously constrained by the small number of items it could absorb during any single experience, yet Luria found that S had an unlimited capacity to learn details. Luria observed S for nearly thirty years, and concluded that instead of storage S's "recall could more easily be explained in terms of factors governing *perception and attention.*" (Emphasis Luria's.) Of course, attention and recall of perception are the bases of factual memory.

S could recall a list recited a dozen years earlier by an amazing feat of multisensory association. Luria asked about a list and S replied, "Oh, yes. You wore a grey shirt. I can hear you say . . ." and out came the list. He saw it and heard it. An ordinary person might be able to recall an image of someone and say he wore a green sweater. S could do much more. He could recall the sweater, the pants, the eyeglass frames, and the belt-buckle. He saw the person before him with near hallucinatory clarity. Indeed, the richness of S's recall caused him problems, as Jerome Bruner, a cognitive psychologist at Harvard, remarked in his foreword to Luria's book about S. S, said Bruner, had "a memory of particulars. . . . But it is a memory that is particularly lacking in one important feature: the capacity to convert encounters with the particular into instances of the general."

S's inability to generalize was a direct result of his heavy reliance on a powerful factual memory. In our study of forgetting we saw that memory for the general is an imperfect memory of particulars. Generalized knowledge depends on having several similar experiences to which we did not pay enough attention for us to remember the details that set each experience apart. If the memory is too precise, as with me and *punctual*, we get beyond generalities. S's associations were so precise that his memory could seldom divorce an experience from its original context. Of course, everyone finds that some details from past experience are irrelevant to the present situation. It takes insight, a climb to interpretive memory, to distinguish between apt and extraneous associations, but S relied almost exclusively on factual memory and seldom had the insights that would have let him use his rich associations for practical purposes.

He even showed this same reliance on factual memory in his use of language. He understood words purely as triggers for associated perceptions; a word evoked a concrete image or it meant nothing. Words strung together in a sentence evoked multiple images. S did not chunk words into a unified thought. For example, if I said, "He weighed the salami," S would imagine a scale and a salami. He would see each item in all its detail and perhaps even taste the freshly cut salami. This sounds good; I regret that my own imagination is not so rich, but here is what such perception did to him when S discussed the phrase, "to weigh one's words":

> Now how can you weigh words? When I hear the word *weigh* I see a large scale—like the one we had in Rezhitsa in our shop, where they put bread on one side and a weight on the other. The arrow shoots to one side, then stops in the middle. . . . But what do you have here—to *weigh one's words!*

S goes wrong when he says, "When I hear the word *weigh,* I see a large scale." *Weigh* is a verb, an action. No particular thing gets at the meaning. S's vast powers of factual association gave him many examples of things being weighed, but his complete lack of insight made it impossible for him to understand the metaphorical use of the verb.

Problems of this sort would seem impossible in anyone with a properly functioning interpretive memory. Luria makes no direct reference to the Bartlett tradition's focus on meaningful memories, but he does report the way meanings confused S's memory. Luria says that S shared a characteristic that "other people with highly developed capacities for figurative memory [recall of perceptions] exhibit: a tendency to rely exclusively on images and to overlook any possibility of using logical means of recall." S was largely content with his powerful factual memory and seldom used chunks. In one experiment he learned a list that included some names of birds. S was then asked to repeat only the bird names. If he had had simply to recite the list, S would have breezed through the task. But now he had to recall a word and interpret its meaning. This extra memory task made the challenge so distracting that S could not do it.

This lack of understanding showed itself in another way as well: S never made the typical errors of people recalling lists. He did not sometimes recall a synonym instead of the actual word, did not cluster words by category, and did not recall an associate like *salt* instead of *pepper*. When Luria first met S, nearly sixty years ago, the absence of these errors seemed like signs of an exquisite memory, but today we know that ordinary people make these errors because they recall things through their grammatical associations. If S never made these errors, perhaps he had no great capacity for interpreting an experience.

Further hints at this lack of understanding lay in S's memory for numbers. For most people, strings of numbers are the hardest things in the world to recall because they are meaningless and random. S thought them easy to remember, but not because he could spot some secret order to them. On the contrary, if the numbers had any order, he did not notice. One time, when doing a memory act on stage, he had the following numbers to remember;

1 2 3 4
2 3 4 5
3 4 5 6
4 5 6 7 . . .

Of course he could do it, but he never noticed an order to the numbers that could enable anybody to recall this list. For most people, the order pops out at them, but apparently S never perceived a meaningful chunk.

Luria reports that much of the world was a continual mystery to S. Typical of his blindness to the meaning of things was S's response to Luria's first test results. S was amazed to learn that his memory was unusual. Did Luria really mean to say that most people could not remember *everything* they had been told? By the time he met Luria, S was nearly thirty. It is true that people tend to assume that what they find easy is just as easy for others, but long before turning thirty everybody has seen many people forget, misremember, and say, "Oh, I can't remember." S grew up in a city and attended school, and yet he never noticed that other people sometimes had memory problems.

He also had difficulties recognizing some familiar chunks. Some of his difficulties sound like the same problems that programmers face in trying to get computers to recognize faces and voices. A machine may be programmed to respond to certain spoken words, but if a speaker is emotionally tense or has a cold or a frog in his throat the machine may not recognize the spoken words. Similarly, a machine may be programmed to recognize a face, but if a person shows up with a new haircut, a slight weight change, or emotions that affect appearance the machine may fail to recognize the face. S too found that people's appearance and voice changed so much from one time to the next that recognition was hard. Instead of saying, "Oh, you have lost some weight," S was likely to say, "Have we met?"

The richness of S's perceptions kept him focused on his internal experience. Essentially, he was uninterested in any external reality. Memory is useful in guiding actions, but S preferred to stay with his perceptions. Most of us need to act, if only to avoid pain and find pleasure, but S used his visual imagination to replace action. He said, "If I want something to happen, I simply picture it in my mind. I don't have to exert any effort to accomplish it—it just happens." As an example, he remembered as a little boy wishing he could stay in bed. So he imagined that the clock showed some earlier time and then he stayed in bed until his mother came and screamed at him to get up. This feat subverted his strong powers of attention by giving himself a private reality to attend to.

Luria says that S's strangeness rested on a peculiarity of perception known as synesthesia, or colored hearing. Synesthesia occurs when the stimulation of one sense leads to the perception of other sensations. Many people report that they feel a relationship between certain sounds and light (e.g., bass voices, dark shades), but the extent of S's synesthesia was remarkable. Here is Luria's description of S's *sensations* as Luria sounded a single tone:

> S [says he] saw a brown strip against a dark background that had red, tonguelike edges. The sense of taste he experienced was like that of sweet and sour borscht, a sensation that gripped his entire tongue.

These synesthesic descriptions sometimes sound like poetry, as when S said to the Russian psychologist Vygotsky, "What a crumbly yellow voice you have," but S did not speak metaphorically. When he heard Vygotsky speak, S felt a crumbly sensation and saw yellow.

Apparently, S was synesthesic all his life. He never outgrew it, and he told Luria of perceiving synesthesic blurs when he was two or three years old. A "synesthesic blur" was S's perception of fog- or steamlike puffs that obscured his vision. S reported, "When I was about two or three years old I was taught the words of a Hebrew prayer. I didn't understand them, and what happened was that the words settled in my mind as puffs of steam or splashes. . . . Even now I *see* these puffs or splashes when I hear certain sounds." Rather than an unusually rich form of perception, S's synesthesia was a sensory handicap. Like blindness or deafness, it alientated him from certain aspects of experience, but unlike blindness or deafness it provided a hallucinatory substitute for reality. The blind simply do not see. S saw what was not there. He also heard, tasted, and felt things that were not there. These hallucinations distracted him constantly. He told Luria:

> You know there are people who seem to have many voices, whose voices seem to be an entire composition, a bouquet. The late S. M. Eisenstein [the Soviet film maker] had such a voice: listening to him, it was as though a flame with fibers protruding from it was advancing right toward me. I got so interested in his voice, I couldn't follow what he was saying.

It sounds fantastic and artistic, but ultimately it was crippling. The point of Eisenstein's speech lay in his words, not in whatever kaleidoscope S's brain conjured up.

The synesthesia dissociated S from the world about him, and with no practical guidance from interpretive memory his dissociation grew increasingly bizarre. One particularly striking example was in S's remark about music: "You know why they have music in restaurants? Because it changes the taste of everything. If you select the right kind of music, everything tastes good. Surely people who work in restaurants know this." It is easy to believe that S is onto something very right with this comment, but then you realize he is speaking literally and, at bottom, misses the whole point of music in a restaurant. Food does taste better when you are happy, your company is happy, and you are surrounded by happy strangers. But S is not talking about emotion or fellowship. He is talking about what is on his tongue.

S seems to have been at John Dean's opposite extreme. Dean was a hard man to arouse. S, on the other hand, was aroused by everything, perhaps because his synesthesia made everything so remarkable. His arousal had a different role from ordinary attention. Most people come to attention to learn something about the world, but S often was content simply to perceive it. The sensuous richness of his perceptions became an end in itself and disturbed the functioning of all his memory levels. Emotionally, he was not much interested in the world around him, yet he wished to revel in his perceptions. That lone ambition kept him endlessly aroused without leading to action. For S much of life was one long orientation reaction.

If we accept the old assumption that the purpose of memory is to recall the past as accurately as possible, we must conclude that S's memory was a very good one. His associations with past experiences were so rich and singular that he could remember almost anything. But Luria insisted that despite his wondrous recall S was only a marginally functioning individual. As a guide to action, S's memory did not work well. Luria reports that S was an unusually passive man, always waiting for great things to happen to him but never doing anything to promote them.

Instead of becoming physically energetic, S became an athlete of subjective actions. Even his creative and problem-solving efforts relied on perceptual experiences rather than on symbolic constructions. Mathematics seems completely abstract, but S could solve math problems by imagining them in concrete form. He conjured up enormous images that were irrelevant to the mathematics, but which he could manipulate mentally to solve a problem. If, to be extremely simple, you asked him, "I have ten kopecks and you take four, how many do I have left?" S could immediately imagine your hand holding ten kopecks. He would see the rings on your fingers and the lines of your palm. He would see the marks on the coins, the dates, and the places where use had worn them thin. He would mentally remove four kopecks from that hand and see that six remained. This technique enabled him mentally to solve problems that, in formal algebra, call for up to two equations. The solution had a price. Instead of learning the grammar of the real world, he learned only how to manipulate his private one.

These abilities sufficed to let S function, although not brilliantly. He had a wife and child, and he earned a living. Luria talks only briefly about S's jobs and does not tell why he left them. It tickles my prejudices to think of a newspaper reporter in Stalin's Russia who never noticed the implication of anything that happened around him and who did not understand phrases like *to weigh one's words*, but perhaps he was too literal even for Stalinist editors. He also worked briefly as an efficiency expert, although from the little Luria tells about that experience it sounds as though S's ideas were more imaginative than efficient.

Eventually S found work that suited him—working as a memory expert on stage. Movie fans will remember Mr. Memory in Alfred Hitchcock's *The Thirty-nine Steps*. A performer stood on stage while a rowdy audience called out challenges to his memory. S had a similar act. In one part of his show, audiences cried out things for him to remember and later he would repeat those items in order. Astonishingly, S had invented on his own the same system of artificial memory that the ancients used. To help him in his act, S imagined a space (mostly streets from his childhood) and filled the area with images used as reminders to recall items on a list or, once, even to memorize several stanzas of Dante's *Divine Comedy* in the original Italian, a language S did not speak. Luria seems never to have heard of this method before and describes the system in amazed detail.

Although the stage show sounds perfect for him, S found that he needed new techniques to improve the accuracy of his recall. He never made the typical errors of recall, but sometimes he omitted something from his recital. His errors typified problems of artificial memory. For example, if he had to recall an egg, he might imagine an egg against a white wall, but then as he "walked by" he would overlook the egg because its color blended in with the wall. Errors like that were acceptable in Luria's lab, but not on the stage of a professional Mr. Memory. Only after he began his work as a stage performer did S begin to struggle to master his objective actions. In the rough-and-tumble atmosphere of vaudeville and music halls you have to hallucinate pretty hard to turn a flop into success. Boos and catcalls lie as near as a slip of the tongue, and despite his splendid onstage memory S felt terrified. In his effort to perform well he slowly developed a good useful memory.

First S reinvented the classic techniques for recalling the details of an imaginary perception, practices like including good lighting in the scene (no dark corners) and keeping the images big so he could see them easily. These ideas appear in the *Ad Herennium* and if either S or Luria had known about that ancient book S might have improved his act more quickly; however, S gained one important benefit from finding these secrets by himself. He had been passive all his life, but now S had begun seeking ways to improve his public performance. For the first time in his life he seemed to be asking himself seriously the fundamental question of what to do.

Something new had come into S's life. He wanted something from the outside world: success as a performer. The story Luria tells of S's effort to improve his act describes a person who slowly learns to use a memory staircase for practical purposes. First, S reinvented the *Ad Herennium*'s classic techniques for accurate recall. He bothered with these improvements only when accuracy began to matter to him. Then he gained control over his powers of selective attention. S had always paid attention to as much as possible, but he was no Sherlock Holmes digesting the world in order to discover clues about its secrets, and when he turned to remembering for practical purposes he found that the richness of his imagery created problems. Originally S created complex images for his memory walk, but this work proved too fatiguing. He had to settle for simpler images in his space. Instead of imagining a rich perception with all its physical details, his images grew increasingly schematic and general. Luria reports that S began to get control over his attention. Originally he was alert to everything and when he tried to remember only key points he imagined a screen that blocked most details from view. But eventually he developed the ability to focus his attention, observing only selected parts of an experience.

Gaining control over his attention proved crucial to gaining control over his act. S's compulsion to perceive everything had left him with a peculiar memory problem, an inability to forget. Once a performance ended, S never again needed to know the lists and charts used in that particular show; however, old lists haunted his memory and even threatened to confuse his act. He had to concentrate hard during a performance to remember only the current list. He tried to develop techniques for forgetting, to no avail.

He needed to get a grip on his imagination so that he could recall only what a performance demanded. After he gained practical control over his factual memory he still needed to focus his emotional memory so that it served practical rather than purely subjective ends. Instead of the indiscriminate arousal he had favored in the past, he needed to be alert to the needs of his performance. As always, a practical emotional memory depends on having practical desires. As S told Luria:

One evening—it was the 23rd of April—I was quite exhausted from having given three performances and was wondering how I'd ever get through the fourth. There before me I could see the charts of numbers appearing from the first three perform-ances. It was a terrible problem. I thought: I'll just take a quick look and see if the first chart of numbers is still there. I was afraid somehow that it wouldn't be. I both did and didn't want it to appear. . . . And then I thought: the chart of numbers isn't turning up now and it's clear why—it's because I don't want it to! Aha! That means if I don't want the chart to show up it won't. And all it took was for me to realize this! At that moment I felt I was free. The realization that I had some guarantee against making mistakes gave me more confidence. I began to speak more freely, could even permit myself the luxury of pausing when I felt like it, for I knew that if I didn't want an image to appear, it wouldn't. I felt simply wonderful.

The story of S's memory is a curious inversion of the more familiar memory tale. In the ordinary telling we hear about a person, usually a student, who could never remember anything.

School was so boring. If the story has a happy ending, the scholar discovers the joys of learning, begins to pay attention, and finds that his memory suddenly works perfectly well. S's story tells of a man who could never forget anything, as the whole of experience seemed endlessly remarkable. But there is a happy ending. S discovered the joys of performing and began to pay attention to what could help his behavior. After years of remembering everything no matter what, he suddenly found that he had adapted his memory to the needs of his actions. At last he had made himself the master rather than the slave of memory.

19

THE INTERPRETIVE MEMORY OF MARCEL PROUST

Fragments of existence withdrawn from time . . . this contemplation . . . was the only genuine and fruitful pleasure that I had known.

—Proust, *Time Regained*, 1927

Early in 1909 a scarcely-known French writer named Marcel Proust underwent an emotional and intellectual experience that led him to put aside the philosophical essay he was drafting and begin work on a novel. The new work soon became the passion of his life. Proust had been a frequent visitor to the salons of the Parisian aristocrats of blood and aristocrats of the arts, but he retreated to a sound-proofed room in his home and wrote. Formerly he had passed his summers by the seaside, but he reduced that time and eventually abandoned those excursions altogether. In place of these social habits he wrote and rewrote his epic. The work grew longer, ultimately tripling in size from its original draft. The thousands of pages that Proust wrote were published as seven novels in a series called *Remembrance of Things Past*, although a more accurate translation would be *In Quest of Lost Times*. The books stand as the greatest literary expression of the role of memory in a person's life.

The work that Proust wrote in the silent isolation of his room is difficult to recommend to strangers. Personally, I never read anything that shocked me more with a continuing recognition of experiences. To me, somehow this bizarre hermit has touched exactly on my own feeling, observation, and intellect, but I am a little weird myself. Proust's style runs to long detailed sentences filled with obscure allusions, like this one:

> And Swann felt a very cordial sympathy with the sultan Mahomet II whose portrait by Bellini he admired, who, on finding that he had fallen madly in love with one of his wives, stabbed her to death in order, as his Venetian biographer artlessly relates, to recover his peace of mind.

Even many people who like these fifty-one words find that reading three thousand pages of this is like trying to live for a season on a diet of the world's most exquisite chocolate. This style of writing also made it difficult for Proust to find a publisher. One letter of rejection complained that nobody wanted to read thousands of words about the way Proust turned over in bed. This commonplace view proved correct enough. In my own days as a bookseller I used to see a steady trickle of sales of Proust's volume one. Volume two sold a copy every few months. Volume seven would have been a good place to hide my money. Nobody ever picked it up, let alone went off with it.

Despite the rather specialized appeal of Proust's style and setting, people interested in the relation between memory and life should at least be aware of Proust's epic. He describes the workings of memory that we have seen in this book, and always he puts the matter in the context of human experience. That long account of tossing in bed, for example, is filled with descriptions of motor associations. Science still does not know much about motor associations—except that babies soon learn to suck their thumbs and that even cabbage butterflies hone their reflexes. Proust knew that at this level memory is pure disorientation and that most people struggle desperately to reorient themselves:

> . . . in my own bed . . . I lost all sense of the place in which I
> had gone to sleep, and when I awoke in the middle of the
> night, not knowing where I was, I could not even be sure at
> first who I was; I had only the most rudimentary sense of
> existence, such as may lurk and flicker in the depth of an
> animal's consciousness . . . then the memory—not yet of the
> place in which I was, but of the various other places where I
> had lived and might now very possibly be—would come like a
> rope let down from heaven to draw me out of the abyss of not-
> being.

So Proust too saw memory as the way to climb toward consciousness and would have understood immediately the implications of S's preference for imagining a different clock while in
bed.

We are lucky in Proust. Science often runs ahead of language, leaving us unable to find words to discuss the implications
of the new. We saw how computers caught our language by
surprise and left us with confusing puns. But Proust had so
profound an understanding of his own experience with memory
that, as we arrive at our revolution in memory theory, we find a
classic of literature stands ready to help us think and talk about
what we have learned. Through the narrative voice that Proust
calls "Marcel" readers find an account of memory in the life of
an individual, and at the end of his many millions of words the
reader leaves Proust's novels with an unshakable perception of
memory's contribution to the core of all human experience.

Although written between 1909 and 1922—well before Bartlett, Piaget, and Arnold's memory work—the books assert absolutely that memory has many levels and that each level enriches the meaning of one's experience. Proust's account also
distinguishes between "voluntary" and "involuntary" memory.
Voluntary memory is akin to recall, whereas involuntary memory is closer to recognition, especially emotional recognition.

The story in the novels tells of Marcel's climb up memory's
staircase. As the work opens, Marcel is in bed and the details of
his past affect him only in the disorientation that accompanies

his motor associations. Then he eats a madeleine and suddenly remembers the emotions of his childhood. Before the madeleine, Marcel had thought of memory as the sterile recall of the past—images without the essence of experience—but he changes his mind when he discovers that emotional reminders can move him. Recognition has made him feel connected to his whole life and to the places and people he has known.

The encounter with the madeleine is the book's most famous description of memory at work and of Marcel's refusal to settle for less than the fullness of memory. With his first taste he undergoes an enormous emotional response and quickly swallows more tea, but that does not increase his joy. "It is plain that the truth I am seeking lies not in the cup but in myself. The drink has called it into being, but can only repeat indefinitely, with a progressive diminution of strength, the same message." Proust here gives us a splendid statement of the relation between reminder and memory. The reminder is out there in the environment, and memory cannot work without it, but the effects of the reminder are nowhere in the reminder itself. Language that looks to the reminder (sometimes known as the stimulus, trigger, or even input) to explain the reaction looks in the wrong direction. Studying the reminder is like trying to understand a pointing finger by following it to the wrist. You must forget the hand and look toward where it points.

Marcel refuses to settle for the emotion that the experience evokes, saying, "I put down the cup and examine my own mind." Contrast that refusal to settle with John Dean's taste for embracing positive emotions without prying into their causes. Marcel describes the source of such hesitation: "What an abyss of uncertainty, whenever the mind feels overtaken by itself; when it, the seeker, is at the same time the dark region through which it must go seeking. . . . Seek? More than that: create. It is face to face with something that does not yet exist . . . which it alone can bring into the light of day."

Here at last we have a clear articulation of the fear all of us know when faced with really having to remember something. The uncertain discovery of oneself accompanies a climb up memory's steps. No wonder John Dean balked at climbing. But Marcel was made of bolder stuff and pressed on. "I ask my mind to make one further effort, to bring back once more the fleeting sensation. . . . Ten times over I must essay the task, must lean down over the abyss. And each time the cowardice that deters us from every difficult task, every important enterprise, has urged me to leave the thing alone, to drink my tea and think merely of the worries of today. . . . And suddenly the memory revealed itself. The taste was that little piece of madeleine which . . . my aunt Leone used to give me."

Finally he has climbed to factual memory's level. When we talk about memory we must never ignore how active a process remembering is, how tempting it is to avoid its uncertainties. When we understand that, we can find it easier to think about John Dean. His contentment with emotional memory seems like a terrified turning away from an uncertain truth.

Having reached factual memory, a mass of associations leapt to Marcel's mind and he recalled the images of his boyhood village. But there is more to remember. "I did not yet and must long postpone the discovery of why this memory made me so happy." Before he can climb to that insight he must thoroughly explore the factual level. There we see the difference between the memory of S and of Marcel. S was content with the factual level and did not bother to explore its meaning. Marcel, after struggling to reach the factual level, explores it thoroughly in the hope of finding the reason for his emotion.

The madeleine incident comes at the start; the insight into its source of joy comes at the end. The middle million words explore experience and memory. It is not easy to speak of a plot in Proust because the critical changes are usually alterations in point of view or understanding. Marcel is forever learning that he had misunderstood matters, so instead of describing events that change the plot, Proust shows us Marcel learning things that change his attitude. Barely 300,000 words into the story, a painter called Elstir spells out for Marcel and the readers just what kind of adventure story we are reading. "We do not receive wisdom,'' Elstir says. ''We must discover it for ourselves, after a journey through the wilderness which no one else can make for us, which no one can spare us, for our wisdom is the point of view from which we come at last to regard the world.'' Marcel's story tells of his long journey toward his own wisdom.

Memory is important in this story because it changes as Marcel changes. Meanwhile, forgetfulness leads to blunders: As an adolescent just learning the ways of social custom Marcel goes to a small party during the course of which he receives a sealed envelope. He has no idea what to do with the thing and shoves it into his pocket for surreptitious reading at an opportune moment. Then he forgets all about it and remembers receiving it only when, back home, he finds it in his pocket. Opening the envelope he reads the name of the party guest he should have escorted into the dining room. Oops.

Although the richness of memory is necessary for the development of a personal vision, the story does not mechanically assume that more memory is best. Marcel refers often to memory's cruelty in letting us imagine what we do not want to see or remember some anguish we would prefer to forget. He also shows how memory can lead us to treat a new circumstance as though it were an old one and how we must sometimes forget all of a memory's levels before we can free ourselves of old habits. His great example of ending a memory is in the loss of love, when what made him happiest has gone forever. A long sequence (200+ pages) recounts Marcel's grief at the death of a lover he calls Albertine. The grief and recovery from it are a process of memory. At first, everything reminded Marcel of the dead Albertine. The pattern of raindrops evoked a specific image of Albertine, and that image triggered desire. The impossibility of the desire led to renewed sadness and suffering. Then, when the grief seemed done, when experiences no longer triggered associated images, or if they did, the images no longer evoked desire, Marcel found he still had not done with memory. Motor associations persist. The last thing we forget of love is how to embrace our lover:

> . . . the love of Albertine had disappeared from my memory.
> But it seems that there exists too an involuntary memory of
> the limbs, a pale sterile imitation of the other, but longer lived.
> . . . Our legs and our arms are full of torpid memories.

In this account of the need to retreat from the fullness of
Marcel's memory for Albertine we gain ways of thinking and
talking sympathetically about Dean's contentment with partial
memory. He shunned a rich memory's cruelty.

Albertine's death is the closest the book ever comes to a
typical plot device. The objective world has changed and the
hero must adapt to that change. In this case Marcel adapts by
forgetting the love he once had. The long descent back down the
staircase has ended his pain, but it has also returned him to that
state of disoriented uncertainty about how to act. Forgetting
Albertine was necessary, but like the time he forgot about the
envelope in his pocket, Marcel does not know what he should
do.

Then one day memory comes to Marcel's rescue. The
story's climax unites three experiences of emotional recognition
and factual recall, one after the other, in such rapid succession
that it seems as though the whole of his life has become a single
chunk of memory. The incidents themselves are each as trivial
as tasting a madeleine. One incident is the feel of a slightly
uneven stone in the pavement, which reminds him of Venice.
Second, a servant knocks a spoon against a plate and the sound
reminds him of a railway journey. Third, he wipes his mouth
with a stiff linen napkin and he remembers his arrival at the
seaside town of Balbec where he first met Albertine. These
memories bring all levels together. The emotions of Venice,
Balbec, and the railway are included, as are the images associated with each place, and so too are the meanings of those
memories. Despite their intensity, they never disorient Marcel,
never make him lose contact with where he is. Instead, the many
moments of his past have bent around to unite and become part
of the present. He feels again, as he had with the madeleine,
that he has come face to face with a truth, a truth not lessened

by the fact that it is his own truth, one that no one else in the world would recognize. Marcel has found truth in a madeleine and in the feel of two paving stones. We readers would not find truth in either experience, but each of us can find it somewhere, in something ordinary that reminds us of the reality of our own experience.

Because truth is based as deeply in its subjective meaning as in the objective facts of the situation "what another person sees of a universe . . . is not the same as our own." Marcel's discovery of a world of profoundly individual truths and intimate meanings could be a terrifying discovery of isolation. As Marcel says, the expression of one's truth requires "courage of many kinds, including the courage of one's emotions." He uses that last phrase in exactly the way we speak of having the courage of one's convictions. It takes a commitment to the truth of one's own experience in order to stand by what one feels, just as it does to stand by what one thinks. Without that commitment a person cannot go on to the other discoveries that memory brings, but because of this courage people have found their own truths and discovered ways to translate their visions into reality:

> . . . instead of seeing one world only, our own, we see that world multiply itself and we have at our disposal as many worlds as there are original artists, worlds more different from one another than those which revolve in infinite space.

Marcel's experience with the moments of his past fades, of course, but the insight the experience has given him stays. As Elstir promised a million or so words earlier, the emotions, facts, and insights Marcel has gained have become his wisdom. His journey in the wilderness is done.

For memory students, this story suggests a way for us to start talking about the full experience of memory. The metaphors left over from the artificial-memory tradition are dead for us. Their modernized clothes in computer-technology jargon are no more alive. Instead, we must begin to talk of active creation, of the abyss we face as we explore the darkness within ourselves, of the terror over memory's uncertainty, and of the hard and persistent exploration needed to bring us beyond facts to understanding.

Most people do not want even to read Proust, let alone be like him, and it is not a self-evident principle that private truths are preferable to the wisdom of the group. Neither S nor John Dean wanted such a private revelation, but in Proust's life and memory we see a clear illustration of the human possibility of discovering and developing one's own insights and understanding.

Proust's friends and acquaintances during his long literary apprenticeship would probably have been startled to think he would become memory's most articulate prophet, for Proust recalled details imprecisely. He filled his books with quotations cited from memory, and he almost always got the quotation wrong. Today, we tend to think that anyone who remembers even that there is a verse to quote has a good memory, but Proust was schooled a century ago, and by those standards his recall was not of the best. He forgot people's names and the details or even the broad outlines of important events. Proust acknowledged his poor memory, but he found a silver lining to the cloud, asserting, "Infirmity alone makes us take notice and learn. . . . A little insomnia is not without its value in making us appreciate sleep. . . . An unfailing memory is not a very powerful incentive to the study of the phenomenon of memory."

If we think of memory as a guide to action instead of a storehouse of information, however, Proust's life shows that he had a splendid memory. John Dean's memory gave us an example of someone leaping without looking. In S we saw the opposite problem: endless looking without ever leaping. Proust developed the whole ability to look, remember, and then leap in a successful way. All three levels of memory served him well.

Like Dean, Proust's emotional memory was in fine order. He knew his likes and dislikes, and he acted upon them. From an early age Proust wanted to be a great writer and made that ambition the focus of his life. Of course, original writing cannot rest on emotional memory alone. The expression of a personal vision demands higher levels than this one.

Like S, Proust was also a great observer. His factual memory was subject to the many errors that come from the intrusions of meaningful associations, but he paid attention to many things and had the reputation of taking in every detail around him. Originally he limited his observations chiefly to the social world. During the 1890s he was found regularly attending and observing the most exclusive salons of Paris. At the turn of the century, however, Proust was inspired by reading the art critic John Ruskin to take the buildings and places of the world with the same seriousness he had taken society, and he began paying close attention to the details of everyday experience. The result of all this looking appears in the endless detail of his writing. It is hard to believe that S himself could have told a story more rich in precise and intricate detail.

Unlike Dean and S, however, Proust also understood the implications of events around him. His interpretive memory was in fine shape; yet it took him a long time to begin his great project. Insights can be entirely personal, but many of them make people more like everybody else. For example, in the case of the boy who had an insight that let him say *wait for it to dry,* the development enabled the child to think more like other English speakers. Proust as a boy and adolescent absorbed the richness of French culture and knew he wanted to be a writer, but it took him a long time to develop a unique wisdom. He published a volume of stories when he was in his twenties, but he was more ambitious than productive. Like many young writers (and not a few older ones) his ambition to write a great book was clearer than what his subject matter should be.

He was particularly hard pressed because the literary theories of his day did not grant much authority to the emotional and interpretive levels of memory in which Proust excelled. French philosophy especially has long made great distinction between mind and body, intellect and passion. The novelist who dominated France when Proust came of age (1890s) was Emile Zola, a writer who focused on detail with a scientist's precision, but

Zola believed that emotion and meaning were completely divorced from the facts of one's own life. There was no room for subjectivity in his psychology.

The leading French philosopher of that era was Henri Bergson, a teacher of Proust and husband to one of Proust's cousins. Bergson believed in the importance of subjectivity, but his philosophy was the flip side of Zola's. For Bergson too, the mind and body were divorced, but whereas Zola had concentrated on the body, Bergson's philosophy focused on the mind.

For Proust, who observed facts as deeply as Zola, but who also credited emotion and interpretation with as much importance as did Bergson, the question of what to write about seemed endlessly difficult. He was equally interested in mind and body and needed to find a way to contain the two at once. Thus, the story of his life into his late thirties is a tale of endless preparation. Proust wrote constantly, but published only a little of it. He practiced and perfected his style. He observed, observed, observed. But his subject continued to elude him. He made several false starts on his novel and after long efforts at writing put the drafts aside forever.

Late in 1908 he began writing a philosophical essay, *Contre Sainte-Beuve*. In it Proust articulated his theory that novels should present the remembered details of everyday life. It is in these details, he argued, that we can find the deep truths to which habit makes us blind. In hindsight it seems that Proust had already found his subject—memory and the everyday—but he still had not found a way for his artistic imagination to chunk the pieces together. Then in January 1909 he had some tea and a biscuit (transformed into a madeleine in his story). That afternoon Proust underwent the experience that proved to be the turning point of his life. Emotion and detail came together, and he had his subject. He knew how to talk about intellect and passion at the same time. The two are united by the experiences that give them their personal meaning. For Proust, imagination and memory had suddenly become the same thing.

SOURCE NOTES

AND

INDEX

Sources

A. The Top Twenty-five

Any further reading about memory should begin with the following books. Each is the product of intense thought *and* inquiry.

Anderson, J. R. & Bower, G. H. (1973). *Human associative memory*. Washington: Winston.

Aristotle. *The Treatises*. Including *On memory and reminiscence*.

Arnold, M. B. (1984). *Memory and the brain*. Hillsdale, NJ: Lawrence Erlbaum Associates.

Augustine (1961). *Confessions*. Trans. Pine-Coffin, R. S. New York: Penguin Books.

Baddeley, A. D. (1976). *The psychology of memory*. New York: Basic Books.

Bartlett, F. C. (1932). *Remembering*. Cambridge: Cambridge University Press.

Bolles, E. B. (1982). *So much to say*. New York: St. Martin's Press.

Breuer, J. & Freud, S. (1895). *Studies on hysteria*. Trans. A. Strachey & J. Strachey. In *The standard edition of the complete psychological works of Sigmund Freud,* ed. J. Strachey, vol. 2, 1955. London: Hogarth Press.

Ebbinghaus, H. (1913). *Memory,* trans. D. H. Ruyer & C. E. Bussenius. New York: Teachers College Press.

Erdelyi, M. H. (1985). *Psychoanalysis: Freud's cognitive psychology*. New York: W. H. Freeman.

Freud, S. (1898). *The psychical mechanism of forgetfulness*. In *The standard edition,* ed. & trans., J. Strachey, vol. 3, 1955. London: Hogarth Press.

Freud, S. (1910). *Five lectures on psycho-analysis.* In *The standard edition,* ed. & trans., James Strachey, vol. 11. London: Hogarth Press.

Freud, S. (1959). *An autobiographical study*. In *The standard edition,* ed. & trans., James Strachey, vol. 20. London: Hogarth Press.

Freud, S. (1960). *The psychopathology of everyday life,* trans. A. Tyson, ed. James Strachey. New York: W. W. Norton.

James, W. (1890). *The principles of psychology*. New York: Henry Holt.

Klatzky, Roberta L. (1980). *Human memory: Structures and processes*. New York: W. H. Freeman.

Kolb, B. & Whishaw, Ian Q. (1985). *Fundamentals of human neuro-psychology*. (2nd edition) New York: W. H. Freeman.

Nauta, Walle J. H. & Feirtag, Michael (1986). *Fundamental neuroanatomy*. New York: W. H. Freeman.

Olton, D. S., Gamzu, E. & Corkin, S. (eds) (1985). Memory dysfunctions: An integration of animal and human research from preclinical and clinical perspectives. *Annals of the New York Academy of Sciences,* vol. 444.

Piaget, J. & Inhelder, B. (1973). *Memory and intelligence*. Collab. with Sinclair-de Zwart, H., trans. A. J. Pomerans. New York: Basic Books.

Proust, M. (1981). *Remembrance of things past,* trans. C. K. S. Moncrieff & T. Kilmartin. New York: Ramdom House.

Sacks, O. (1985). *The man who mistook his wife for a hat and other clinical tales*. New York: Summit Books.

Spence, J. D. (1984). *The memory palace of Matteo Ricci*. New York: Viking Press.

Squire, L. R. (1986). Mechanisms of memory. *Science,* 232, 1612-19.

Yates, F. A. (1966). *The art of memory*. London: Routledge and Kegan Paul.

B. Chapter Notes

These notes are organized by chapter in the hope that readers can obtain information quickly without having to do too much searching. Partial references, in the form of Name (date), are listed fully either at the top of the entry for that particular chapter or in part A (The Top Twenty-five) of these listings. Some chapters also include "see also" listings for further reading.

PART ONE—THE REMEMBRANCE OF THINGS PERSONAL

Chapter 1—Does Memory Matter?

4—Hume, D. (1902). *Enquiries concerning the human understanding and concerning the principles of morals*. ed. L. A. Selby-Bigge. Oxford: Clarendon Press, section vi, part i, p. 241.

4—man who could recite Virgil backward, cited in Yates (1966), p. 16.

5—memory is of little value, Norman, D. A. (1969). *Memory and attention: an introduction to human information processing*. New York: John Wiley & Sons, p. 1.

7—lawyer's introductory image, quoted in Yates, p. 11.

8—use of paper in fourteenth-century London, Coleman, J. (1981). *Medieval Readers and Writers: 1350–1400*. New York: Columbia University Press, p. 161.

9—Peter of Ravenna's popularity, Yates (1966), p. 112.

11—Augustine on paradox of memory, Augustine (1961), p. 225.

14—Bacon's rejection of memory, Spence (1984), p. 13.

15—Freud's personal reference, Freud (1960), pp. 24-25.

17—the discussion of the evolution of recognition takes its examples from Wilson, E. O. (1975). *Sociobiology: the new synthesis*. Cambridge, MA: Belknap Press of Harvard University Press: ants, p. 203; fish, p. 203; auks and terns, p. 204.

20—newborn elephant quotation, Douglas-Hamilton, I. & O. (1975). *Among the elephants*. New York: Viking Press, p. 90.

20—account of N'Dume in quicksand, *Ibid.*, p. 92.

21—kitty-cat quote, Becker, J. D. (1973). A Model for the encoding of experiential information. In Schank, R. C. & K. M. Colby (1973). *Computer models of thought and language*. San Francisco: W. H. Freeman and Company, p. 398.

Chapter 2—Memory at Work

See: Bower, G. H. (1981). Mood and Memory. *American Psychologist*, 36: 129-48.

Cohen, N. J., Eichenbaum, H., Deacedo, B. S. & Corkin, S. (1985). Different memory systems underlying acquisition of procedural and declarative knowledge. In Olton et al (1985).

Chapter 3—Emotional Memory

30—Proust's sudden exquisite pleasure, Proust (1981), vol. 1, p. 46.

31—Arabs look up hatreds in memory, Schank, R. C. (1982). *Dynamic Memory: a theory of reminding and learning in computers and people*. New York: Cambridge University Press, p. 116.

33—Proustian experience among rabbits, Ketty, S. S. (1976). Biological concomitants of affective states and their possible role in memory processes. In M. R. Rosenzweig & E. L. Bennett (eds). *Neural mechanisms of learning and memory*. Cambridge, MA: MIT Press, p. 323.

36—Little Albert study, Watson, J. B. & Rayner, R. (1920). Conditioned emotional reactions. *Journal of Experimental Psychology*, 3: 1-14.

38—cabbage butterfly memory, Lewis, A C. (1986). Memory constraints and flower choice in pieris rapae. *Science*, 232: 863-65.

39—theory of circular reactions is developed in, Piaget, J. (1952). *The Origins of intelligence in children*, trans., M. Cook. New York: International Universities Press. See also: Piaget, J. (1951). *Plays, dreams, and imitation in childhood*, trans., C. Gattegno & F. M. Hodgson. New York: W. W. Norton. Piaget, J. (1954). *The construction of reality in the child*. New York: Basic Books.

See also: Evans, R. I. (1968). *B. F. Skinner: the man and his ideas*. New York: E. P. Dutton & Co.

Chapter 4—Factual Memory

See: Lynn, R. (1966). *Attention, arousal and the orientation reaction*. Oxford: Pergamon Press.

48—Fan effects discussed in Reder, L. M. & Wible, C. (1984). Strategy use in question-answering: Memory strength and task constraints on fan effects. *Memory and Cognition*.

48—importance of attention, James (1890), p. 427.

49—definition of attention, *Ibid.*, p. 403.

49—for good memory of high arousal words, Kleinsmith, L. J. & Kaplan, S. (1963). Paired associate learning as a function of arousal and interpolated interval. *Journal of Experimental Psychology*, 65: 190-93; for corroborating research see Kleinsmith, L. J. & Kaplan, S. (1964). Interaction of arousal and recall interval in nonsense syllable and paired-associate learning. *Journal of Experimental Psychology*, 67: 124-26; Walker, E. & Tarte, R. D. (1963). Memory storage as a function of arousal and time with homogeneous and hetrogeneous lists. *Journal of Verbal Learning and Verbal Behavior*, 2: 113-19; Corteen, R. S. (1969). Skin conductance changes and word recall. *British Journal of Psychology*, 60: 80-4; Butter, M. J. (1970). Differential recall of pair associates as a function of arousal and concreteness-imagery levels. *Journal of Experimental Psychology*, 84: 252-56; McClean, P. D. (1969). Induced arousal and time of recall as determinants of paired-associate recall. *British Journal of Psychology*, 60: 57-62.

50—for a survey of the nature of the orientation reaction, Lynn (1966).

50—Pavlov on the origin of inquisitiveness, Pavlov, I. P. (1927). *Conditioned reflexes*. Oxford: Blackwell. p. 12.

51—differences in habituation, Lynn (1966), pp. 6-7.

51—main sources on recency effect, Glanzer, M. & Meinzer, A. (1967). The effects of intralist activity on free recall. *Journal of Verbal Learning and Verbal Behavior*, 6: 928-35; Craik, F. I. M. (1968). Two components in

free recall. *Journal of Verbal Learning and Verbal Behavior,* 7: 996-1004;
Craik, F. I. M. & Levy, B. A. (1970). Semantic and acoustic information
in primary memory. *Journal of Experimental Psychology,* 86: 77-82.

53—result of incidental learning, Baddeley, A. D. & Hitch, G. (1976). Recency
reexamined. In S. Dornic (ed), *Attention and Performance,* VI.

58—screen memories, Freud, S. (1899). Screen memories. In *The standard
edition,* ed. & trans., James Strachey. vol 3. London: Hogarth Press.

58—own voice does not confuse auditory prompt recall, Bryden,
M. P. (1971). Attention strategies and short-term memory in dichotic
listening. *Cognitive Psychology* 2: 99-116.

59—experiment on recency effect counting 20 backwards, Tzeng,
O. J. L. (1973). Positive recency effect in delayed free recall. *Journal of
Verbal Learning and Verbal Behavior,* 12: 436-39. (1973).

61—chunks of unanalyzed famous clichés, Rubin, D. C. (1977). Very long-
term memory for prose and verse. *Journal of Verbal Learning and Verbal
Behavior,* 16: 611-21.

61—child's alteration wait for it to cool, Clark, R. (1974). Performing without
competence. *Journal of Child Language,* 1: 1-10.

See also: Brown, J. A. (1958). Some tests of the decay theory of immediate
memory. *Journal of Experimental Psychology,* 10: 12-21.

Chapter 5—Interpretive Memory

See: Miller, G. A. (1956). The magical number seven, plus or minus two: some
limits on our capacity for processing information. *Psychological Review,*
63: 81-97.

Tulving, E. & Donaldson, W., eds. (1972). *Organization and memory.* New
York: Academic Press.

67—Bartlett's claim that memory and imagination are an expression of the
same activities, Bartlett (1932), p. 214.

68—study of order of approximation, Miller, G. A. & Selfridge, J. A. (1950).
Verbal context and the recall of meaningful material. *American Journal of
Psychology,* 63: 176-87.

70—confused recognition becomes unconfused in organized settings, Mandler,
G., Pearlstone, Z., & Koopmans, H. S. (1969). Effects of organization
and semantic similarity on a recall and recognition task. *Journal of Verbal
Learning and Verbal Behavior,* 8: 410-23.

70—grammatical organization makes confused recognition unlikely, Lachman,
R. & Tuttle, A. V. (1965). Approximation to English and short-term
memory: Construction or storage: *Journal of Experimental Psychology,*
70: 386-93.

71—harmony between recall and recognition, Mandler, G. (1972). Organization
and recognition. In Tulving & Donaldson (1972).

72—Piaget's first principle, Piaget & Inhelder (1973), p. 8.

72—the process of lumping, Tulving, E. (1962). Subjective organization in free recall of "unrelated" words. *Psychological Review,* 69: 344-54.

73—pairing imposed on random lists, Jenkins, J. J. & Russell, W. A. (1952). Associative clustering during recall. *Journal of Abnormal and Social Psychology,* 47: 818-21.

73—first lab evidence of superiority of recognition, McDougall, R. (1904). Recognition and recall. *Journal of Philosophical and Scientific Methods,* 1: 229-33.

74—amnesiacs better at recognition, Hirst, W., Johnson, M. K., Kim, J. K., Phelps, E. A., Risse, G., & Volpe, B. T. (1986). Recognition and recall in amnesics. *Journal of Experimental Psychology: Learning, Memory, and Cognition,* 12: 445-51.

74—experiments with poorer recognition than recall, eg., Bahrick, H. P. & Bahrick, P. O. (1964). A reexamination of the interrelations among measures of retention. *Quarterly Journal of Experimental Psychology,* 16: 318-24.

74—recognition confused by context but recall isn't, Tulving E., & Thompson, D. M. (1973). Encoding specificity and retrieval processes in episodic memory. *Psychological Review,* 80: 352-73; Watkins, M. J. & Tulving, E. (1975). Episodic memory: when recognition fails. *Journal of Experimental Psychology: General,* 104: 5-29; Wiseman, S. & Tulving, E. (1976). Encoding specificity: Relation between recall superiority and recognition failure. *Journal of Experimental Psychology: Human Learning and Memory,* 2: 349-61; Tulving E. & Watkins, O. C. (1977). Recognition failure of words with a single meaning. *Memory & Cognition,* 5: 513-22.

75—chess study, De Groot, A. D. (1965). *Thought and choice in chess.* The Hague: Mouton: De Groot, A. D. (1966). Perception and memory versus thinking. In B. Kleinmuntz (ed.). *Problem solving.* New York: Wiley; Simon. H. A. & Barenfeld, M. (1969). Information-processing analysis of perceptual problems in problem solving. *Psychological Review,* 76: 473-83; Simon, H. A. & Gilmartin, K. (1973). A simulation of memory for chess positions. *Cognitive Psychology,* 5: 29-46.

75—Othello perceived like chess, Wolff, A. S., Mitchell, D. H. & Frey, P. W. (1984). Perceptual skill in the game of Othello. *Journal of Psychology,* 118: 7-16.

76—Piaget's second principle, Piaget & Inhelder (1973), p. 19.

78—for classic paper on chunking see Miller (1956).

86—spatial memory related to foraging requirements, Dale, R. H. & Bedard, M. (1984). Limitations on spatial memory in mice. *Southern Psychologist,* 2: 23-6.

88—remarks by boy who saw but did not understand cork, Piaget & Inhelder (1973), p. 244.

89—Piaget's third principle, *Ibid.,* p. 385.

90—recognition favors the plausible, Reder, L. M. & Wible, C. (1984). Strategy use in question-answering: Memory strength and task constraints on fan effects. *Memory & Cognition,* 12: 411-19.

90—poor recognition for "irrelevant" facts, Dellarosa & Bourne (1984).

See also:

Bahrick, H. P., Bahrick, P. O. & Wittlinger, R. P. (1975). Fifty years of memory for names and faces: a cross-sectional approach. *Journal of Experimental Psychology: General,* 104: 54-75.

Bousefield, W. A. (1953). The occurrence of clustering in recall of randomly arranged associates. *Journal of General Psychology,* 49: 229-40.

Coffer, C. N., Bruce, D., & Reicher, G. M. (1966). Clustering in free recall as a function of certain methodological variations. *Journal of Experimental Psychology,* 71: 858-66.

Cohen, B. H. (1963). Recall of categorized word lists. *Journal of Experimental Psychology,* 66: 227-34.

Coltheart, V. & Winograd, E. (1986). Word imagery but not age of acquisition affects episodic memory. *Memory & Cognition,* 14: 174-80.

Graesser, A. II & Mandler, G. (1978). Limited processing capacity constrains the storage of unrelated sets of words and retrieval from natural categories. *Journal of Experimental Psychology: Human Learning and Memory,* 4: 86-100.

Graf, P. & Mandler, G. (1984). Activation makes words more accessible, but not necessarily more retrievable. *Journal of Verbal Learning and Verbal Behavior,* 23: 553-68.

Mandler, G. (1980). Recognizing: the judgment of previous occurrence. *Psychological Review,* 87: 251-72.

Mandler, G. (1985). From association to structure. *Journal of Experimental Psychology: Learning, Memory, & Cognition,* 11: 464-68.

Mandler, G. & Dean, P. J. (1969). Seriation: development of serial order in free recall. *Journal of Experimental Psychology,* 81: 207-15.

Mandler, G. & Rabinowitz, J. C. (1981). Appearance and reality: Does a recognition test really improve subsequent recall and recognition. *Journal of Experimental Psychology: Human Learning & Memory,* 7: 79-90.

Mandler, G. & Shebo, B. J. (1982). Subitizing: an analysis of its component processes. *Journal of Experimental Psychology: General,* 11: 1-22.

Paivio, A. (1969). Mental imagery in associative learning and memory. *Psychological Review,* 76: 241-63.

Rubin, D. C. & Friendly, M. (1986). Predicting which words get recalled: Measures of free recall, availability, goodness, emotionality, and pronouncability for 925 nouns. *Memory & Cognition,* 14: 79-94.

Tulving, E. (1972). Episodic and semantic memory. In Tulving & Donaldson (1972).

296 / *Sources*

Williams, K. W., & Francis, T. D. (1986). Judging category frequency: automaticity or availability? *Journal of Experimental Psychology: Learning, Memory, and Cognition,* 12: 387-96.

Chapter 6—The Arts of Memory

See:

Bowers, K. & Dywan, J. (1983). The use of hypnosis to enhance recall. *Science,* 222: 184-85.

Orne, M. T., Soskis, D. A., Dinges, D. F., & Orne, E. C. (1984). Hypnotically induced testimony. In Welles & Loftus, eds.

Wells, G. L. & Loftus, E. (Eds.) (1984). *Eyewitness testimony: Psychological perspectives.* Cambridge: Cambridge University Press.

93—Borges on blindness, Gargan, E. A. (1986). Jorge Luis Borges, a master of fantasy and fables, is dead. *New York Times,* June 15, p. A30:4.

95—poll of college students on memory, Orne et al. (1984), p. 175.

96—hypnosis technique requires continual reinforcement, *Ibid.*

97—subjects remember day of week of old birthdays, True, R. M. (1949). Experimental control in hypnotic age regression states. *Science,* 110: 583-84.

97—four-year-olds don't know the day of the week, Orne et al (1984).

97—hypnotist communicated answer to subjects, *Ibid.*

97—hypnosis ceases to aid memory in interviews, *Ibid.*

98—hypnosis radically alters a person's willingness to voice a memory, Bowers & Dywan (1983).

98—recalled version of Village Smithy, Stalnaker, J. M. & Riddle, E. E. (1932). The effect of hypnosis on long-delayed recall. *Journal of General Psychology,* 6: 429-40.

98—hypnosis does not work better than repeated recall, Nogrady, H., McConkey, K. M. & Perry, C. (1985). Enhancing visual memory: Trying hypnosis, trying imagination, and trying again. *Journal of Abnormal Psychology,* 94: 195-204.

98—repeated recall improves memory, Erdelyi, M. H. & Kleinbard, J. (1978). Has Ebbinghaus decayed with time?: The growth of recall (hypermnesia) over days. *Journal of Experimental Psychology: Human Learning and Memory,* 4: 275-89.

99—repeated recall followed by hypnosis leads to confabulation, Bowers & Dywan (1983).

99—hypnotized witnesses are unusually confident about their memory of event, Orne et al. (1984).

99—hypnotism can plant memories, Perry, C. & Laurence, J (1983). Hypnotically created memory among highly hypnotizable subjects. *Science*, 222: 523-24.

99—memory is an imaginative construction, Bartlett (1932), p. 214.

100—precepts for good memories require good memories, Spence (1984), p. 4.

102—artificial memory is too carnal, from Yates (1966).

104—experiment on types of meaningful associations, Bower, G. H. & Winzenz, D. (1970). Comparison of associative learning strategies. *Psychonomic Science*, 20: 119-20.

106—story of Simonides of Ceos opens Yates (1966), pp. 1-2.

107—*Ad Herennium* on bizarre images, from Yates (1966), p. 8.

109—insight leads to memory of list, Katona, G. (1940). *Organizing and memorizing*. New York: Columbia University Press.

109—Descartes on memory, in Yates (1966), p. 373.

See also: Brown, R. & McNeill, D. (1966). The "tip of the tongue" phenomenon. *Journal of Verbal Learning & Verbal Behavior*, 5: 325-37.

Geiselman, R. E., Fisher, R. P., MacKinnon, D. P. & Holland, H. L. (1985). Eyewitness memory enhancement in the police interview: Cognitive retrieval mnemonics versus hypnosis. *Journal of Applied Psychology*, 70: 401-12.

Hall, David F., Loftus, Elizabeth F., & Tougignant, Japes P. (1984). Postevent information and changes in recollection for a natural event. In Wells & Loftus (1984).

Loftus, E. F. & Greene, E. (1980). Warning: even memory for faces may be contagious. *Law and Human Behavior*, 4: 323-34.

Malpass, R. S. & Devine, P. G. (1981). Guided memory in eyewitness identification. *Journal of Applied Psychology*, 66: 343-50.

Shepherd, J. W., Davies, G. M. & Ellis, H. D. (1978). How best shall a face be described? In Grunberg, M. M., Morris, P. E. & Sykes, R. N. (eds) (1978). *Practical aspects of memory*. London: Academic Press.

Shepherd, J. W. & Ellis, H. D. (1973). The effect of attractiveness on recognition memory for faces. *American Journal of Psychology*, 86: 627-33.

Watkins, M. J. (1977). The intricacy of the memory span. *Memory & Cognition*, 5: 529-34.

Wells, G. L. & Hyryciw, B. (1984). Memory for faces: Encoding and retrieval operations. *Memory & Cognition*, 12: 338-44.

Wells, G. L. & Loftus, E. (1984). Eyewitness research: then and now. In Wells & Loftus, Eds. (1984).

Wells, G. L. & Murray, D. M. (1984). Eyewitness confidence. In Wells & Loftus, Eds. (1984).

Winograd, E. (1981). Elaboration and distinctiveness in memory for faces. *Journal of Experimental Psychology: Human Learning and Memory*, 7: 181-90.

PART TWO—THE BIOLOGY OF MEMORY

Chapter 7—Newfound Surprises

117—Lashley's despair of learning, Lashley, K. S. (1951). The problem of serial order in behavior. In Jeffress, L. A., ed. (1951). *Cerebral mechanisms in behavior: The Hixon symposium*. New York: John Wiley. p. 480.

119—John's idea is set forth in John, E. R. (1967). *Mechanisms of memory*. New York: Academic Press.

121—For Pribram's theory and its development see: Pribram, K. H. (1971) *Language of the brain: Experimental paradoxes and principles in neuropsychology*. Englewood cliffs, NJ: Prentice-Hall; Pribram, K. H. (1980). Mind, brain, and consciousness: The organization of competence and conduct. In Davidson, R. J. & Davidson, M. (eds) *The psychology of consciousness*. New York: Plenum Press; Pribram, K. H. (1982). Localization and distribution of function in the brain. In Ohrbach, J. (ed) *Neuropsychology after Lashley*. Hillsdale, NJ: Erlbaum.

122—Atkinson-Shiffrin model of memory presented in, Atkinson, R. L. & Shiffrin, R. M. (1968). Human memory: A proposed system and its control processes. In Spence, K. W. & Spence, J. T. (eds) *The psychology of learning and motivation: Advances in research and theory*, vol. 2. New York: Academic Press.

See also: Bloom, F. E., Lazerson, A. & Hofstadter, L. (1985). *Brain, mind, and behavior*. New York: W. H. Freeman.

Hall, Stephen S. (1985). Aplysia & Hermissenda. *Science 85*. May: 30-39.

Klopf, A. H. (1982). *The hedonistic neuron: A theory of memory, learning, and intelligence*. Washington: Hemisphere Publishing Corp. [Note: I include Klopf's book even though it has much of the crackpot about it, because it introduces the idea of the neuron changing its behavior rather than changing a storehouse.]

Knudsen, E. (1983). Early auditory experience aligns the auditory map of space in the optic tecum of the barn owl. *Science*, 222: 939-42.

Lashley, K. S. (1929). *Brain mechanisms and intelligence: A quantitative study of injuries to the brain*. Chicago: University of Chicago Press.

Nolen, T. G. & Hoy, R. R. (1984). Initiation of behavior by single neurons: The role of behavioral context. *Science*, 226: 992-4.

Chapter 8—The Organ of Memory

See:

Alkon, D. L. (1984). Calcium-mediated reduction of ionic currents: A biophysical memory trace. *Science,* 226: 1037-45.

Reinis, S. & Goldman, J. M. (1982). *The chemistry of behavior: A molecular approach to neuronal plasticity.* New York: Plenum Press.

123—list of ways neuron might change in Woody, C. D. (1982). *Memory, learning, and higher function: A cellular view.* New York: Springer-Verlag.

125—basic work on synapses, Eccles, J. C. (1964). *The physiology of synapses.* New York: Springer-Verlag.

126-sea anemone's doorbell, Nauta & Feirtag (1986), p. 8.

127—Freud to Fliess, Freud, S. (1902). Extracts from the Fliess papers. In *The standard edition,* ed. & trans., James Strachey, vol. 1. London: Hogarth Press, p. 234.

127—Breuer's argument on the separation of neuron and memory, Breuer & Freud (1895), p. 188n.

128—book-length plasticity lists, e.g., Reinis & Goldman (1982).

128—for a discussion of internal neuron changes and implications, see Black, I. B. (1984). Intraneuronal mutability: Implications for memory mechanisms. *Brain, Behavior & Evolution,* 24: 35-46; Finger, S. (1984). Symposium discussion: Paradigms, methodologies, and memory mechanisms. *Physiological Psychology,* 12: 89-91; Kolers, P. A. & Roediger, H. L. (1984). Procedures of mind. *Journal of Verbal Learning & Verbal Behavior,* 23: 425-49.

129—each neuron is distinct quote, Reinis & Goldman (1982), p. 110.

130—percent of barrier neurons in humans, Nauta & Feirtag (1985), p. 38.

130—for survey of sea-snail research, see Alkon (1984).

See also: Dumont, J. P. C. & Robertson, R. M. (1986). Neuronal circuits: An evolutionary perspective. *Science,* 233: 849-53.

Chapter 9—Memory Circuits

139—trillion cells in brain, Nauta & Feirtag (1985).

139—basic discussion of brain based on *Ibid.,* Bloom, F. E., Lazerson, A., & Hofstadter, L. (1985). *Brain, mind, and behavior.* New York: W. H. Freeman; Thompson, R. F. (1985). *The brain: An introduction to neuroscience.* New York: W. H. Freeman & Company.

140—size and recency of cerebral cortex, Nauta & Feirtag (1986), pp. 46-8.

300 / *Sources*

143—split brain study, Gazzaniga, M. S. (1970). *The bisected brain.* New York: Appleton-Century-Crofts.

143—split-brain failure in jigsaw puzzles, Arnold (1984), p. 268.

144—return of respectability of subject of awareness, Burghardt, G. M. (1985). Animal awareness: Current perceptions and historical perspective. *American Psychologist,* 40: 905-19.

144—for fuller information on sensory maps see: Hubel, D. H. & Wiesel, T. N. (1977). Ferrier lecture: Functional architecture of macaque monkey visual cortex. *Proceedings of the Royal Society of London, Series B,* pp. 1-59. See also: Cornsweet, T. N. (1970). *Visual perception.* New York: Academic Press; Van Essen, D. C. & Maunsell, J. H. R. (1983). Hierarchical organization and functional streams in the visual cortex. *Trends in Neurosciences,* 370-75.

147—Korsakoff recognition improves, Warrington, E. K. (1985). A discrimination analysis of amnesia. In Olton et al. (1985).

147—memory circuits theory based on Arnold (1984).

150—cats learn milk but not shock, Arnold (1984), p. 252.

154—thalamus active during memory, John, E. Roy (1967). *Mechanisms of memory.* New York: Academic Press, p. 234, 419.

156—effects of bilateral hippocampus destruction in animals, Arnold (1984), pp. 314-5.

158—amygdala and orientation reaction, *Ibid.,* pp. 223-5.

158—evidence for separate motor memory region, Englekamp, J. & Zimmer, H. D. (1984). Motor programme information as a separable memory unit. *Psychological Research,* 46: 283-99. Zimmer (1984).

158—cerebellum controls learned eye-responses, Thompson, R. F. (1986). The neurobiology of learning and memory. *Science,* 233: 941-47.

158—action of frontal lobotomies, Valenstein, E. S. (1986). *Great and desperate cures: The rise and decline of psychosurgery and other radical treatments for mental illness.* New York: Basic Books.

158—the role of frontal cortex has been widely explored. Some important sources: to disprove role in intelligence, Hebb, D. O. (1939). Intelligence in man after large removals of cerebral tissue: Report of four left frontal lobe cases. *Journal of General Psychology,* 21: 73-87; planning of motion, Roland, P. E., Larsen, B., Lassen, N. A., & Skinhoj, E. (1980). Supplementary motor area and other cortical areas in organization of voluntary movements in man. *Journal of Neurophysiology,* 43: 118-36; spontaneity, Jones-Gotman, M. & Milner, B. (1977). Design fluency: The invention of nonsense drawings after focal cortical lesions. *Neuropsycholgia,* 15: 653-74.

158—same point in frontal cortex controls outcome of motion, even if process of arrival differs, Arnold (1984) p. 185.

160—speech by person sorting cards, Kolb & Whishaw (1985), p. 430.

162—for other work on memory circuits see: Deutsch, J. A. (ed) (1983). *The physiological basis of memory,* 2nd ed. New York: Academic Press; Squire, L. R. & Butters, N., eds. (1984). *Neuropsychology of memory.* New York: Guilford; Brookhart, J. M. & Mountcastle, V. B., eds. (1987). *Handbook of physiology: The nervous system.* Bethesda, MD: American Physiological Society.

163—Memory not an isolated process, Arnold (1984), p. vii.

See also: Cowan, W. M. (1979). The development of the brain. *Scientific American,* September, pp. 106-17.

Crick, F. H. C. (1979). Thinking about the brain. *Scientific American,* September, 241: 219-232.

Chapter 10—Memory Studies Today

164—Squire, L. R. (1986). Mechanisms of memory. *Science,* June 27, pp. 1612-19.

165—memory stored as changes, *Ibid.,* p. 1612.

165—discussion of the history of the word *memory* in computers is based on Shurkin, J. (1984). *Engines of the mind: A history of the computer.* New York: W. W. Norton.

166—first reference to computer memory, von Neumann, J. (1945). First draft of a report on the EDVAC. In Stern, N. (1981). *From ENIAC to UNIVAC: An appraisal of the Eckert-Mauchly computers.* Bedford, MA: Digital Press, p. 183.

167—Eckert quote, Shurkin (1984). p. 172.

167—computer as brain metaphor, *Ibid.,* p. 184.

168—theory of functional similarity, Putnam, H. (1975). *Mind, Language and Reality: Philosophical Papers,* vol. 2. Philosophy and Our Mental Life. Cambridge: Cambridge University Press.

169—creation combines chunks, see e.g., Guilford, J. P. (1959). Three faces of intellect. *American Psychologist,* 14: 469-79; Koestler, A. (1964). *The act of creation.* New York: Dell Publishing Co.

171—memory drugs may be on market in 1980s, Begley, S., Springen, K., Katz, S., Hager, M., & Jones, E. (1986). Memory. *Newsweek,* September 29, pp. 48-54.

171—body promotes amnesia for childbirth pain, Weingartner, H. (1986). The roots of failure. *Psychology Today,* January, pp. 6-7.

172—caffeine research, Snyder, S. (1986). Broadcast interview concerning caffein and memory. "Nightline," ABC television.

172—nicotine helps memory, Peeke & Peeke (1984). Attention, memory, and cigarette smoking. *Psychopharmacology,* 84: 205-16.

172—vasopressin speeds up factual learning, Koob (1985). Koob, G. F., Lebrun, C., Martinez, J. L., Jr., Dantzer, R., LeMoal, M., & Bloom, F. E. (1985). Arginine Vasopressin, Stress, and Memory. In Olton et al. (1985).

172—drug helps memory in males, Beckwith, Till, & Schneider (1984). Beckwith, B. E., Till, & Schneider, V. (1984). Vasopressin analog (DDAVP) improves memory in human males. *Peptides,* 5: 819-22.

175—Neisser, U. (1976). *Cognition and reality: Principles and implications of cognitive psychology.* San Francisco: W. H. Freeman. "Villains of piece," p. 10; "Consciousness is . . . mental activity," p. 105.

See also: Arnsten, A. F. T., & Goldman-Rakic, P. S. (1985). Catecholamines and cognitive decline in aged nonhuman primates. In Olton et al. (1985).

Ghoneim, M. M., Mewaldt, S. P. & Hinrichs, J. V. (1984). Behavioral effects of oral versus intravenous administration of diazepam. *Pharmacology, Biochemistry & Behavior,* 21: 231-6.

Osborn, C. D. & Holloway, F. A. (1984). Can commonly used antibiotics disrupt formation of new memories? *Bulletin of the Psychonomic Society,* 22: 356-58.

Part Three—THE FORGETTERY

Chapter 11—Ordinary "Forgetting"

See: Crovitz, H. F., Cordoni, C. N., Daniel, W. F., & Perlman, J. (1984). Everyday forgetting experiences: Real-time investigations with implications for the study of memory management in brain-damaged patients. *Cortex,* 20: 349-59.

Neisser, Ulric (1976). *Cognition and reality: Principles and implications of cognitive psychology.* San Francisco: W. H. Freeman.

179—people often forget intentions, Crovitz et al. (1984).

182—Freud on forgetting intentions, Freud (1960), p. 153.

183—Freud believed every incident was stored as memory, see e.g. Freud, S. (1900). The interpretation of dreams. In *The standard edition,* ed. & trans., James Strachey. vol. 4. London: Hogarth Press, p. 20.

183—search for attention filters was futile, Neisser (1976) p. 80.

184—next-in-line effect, Bond, C. F. (1985). The next-in-line effect: Encoding or retrieval deficit? *Journal of Personality and Social Psychology,* 48: 853-62.

187—automatic action requires disengagement from reality, Lashley, K. S. (1951). The problem of serial order in behavior. In Jeffress, L. A., ed. (1951). *Cerebral mechanisms in behavior: The Hixon symposium.* New York: John Wiley. [paper presented orally in 1948].

187—basic nature of absentmindedness, Reason, J. (1984). Absentmindedness and cognitive control. In Harris, J. E. & P. E. Morris, eds. (1984). *Everyday memory, actions and absentmindedness.* London: Academic Press.

188—lion learning to hunt, Bartlett, D. & J. (1975). *The Lions of Etosha: King of the Beasts.* Survival Anglia Ltd. [Film] Productions.

189—pitching control depends on concentration, Kaat, J. (1986). Texas Rangers vs. New York Yankees telecast, May 4.

190—for a discussion of shadowing, see Neisser (1976) Chapter 5.

192—absent-mindedness is common, Crovitz et al. (1984).

Chapter 12—Forgotten Chunks

198—sample of R. H.'s speech, Goodglass, H., Gleason, J. B., Bernholtz, N., & Hyde, R. N. (1972). Some linguistic structures in the speech of a Broca's aphasic. *Cortex,* 8: 191-212. (Extract on p. 195.)

199—experiments suggesting aphasics may have limited chunking abilities, Gutbrod, K., Mager, B., Meier, E. & Cohen, R. (1985). Cognitive processing of tokens and their description in aphasia. *Brain & Language,* 25: 37-51.

199—right brain aphasia, Zaidel, E. (1978). Auditory language comprehension in the right hemisphere following cerebral commissurotomy and hemispherectomy: A comparison with child language and aphasia. In Caramazza, A. & Zurif, e.b. (Eds) (1978). *Language acquisition and language breakdown: Parallels and divergencies.* Baltimore: Johns Hopkins University Press.

200—color agnosia vs. color aphasia, Kolb & Whishaw (1985), p. 215.

200—agnosias for faces and illness, *ibid.,* p. 214.

202—word-deaf children ignore television soundtracks, Friedlander, B. Z., Wetstone, H. S., & McPeek, D. L. (1974). Systematic assessment of selective language listening deficit in emotionally disturbed preschool children. *Journal of Child Psychology and Psychiatry,* 15: 1-12.

202—Dr. P's description of a glove, Sacks (1985), p. 13.

203—child whose language did not move beyond factual memory, Blank, M., Gessner, M., & Esposito, A. (1979). Language without communication: A case study. *Journal of Child Language,* 6: 329-52.

204—for survey of forms of dyslexia see Coltheart, M. (1981). Disorders of reading and their implications for models of normal reading. *Visible Language,* XV: 245-86.

See also:

Critchley, M. (1962). Dr. Samuel Johnson's aphasia. *Medical History*, 6: 27-44.

Goodglass, H., Klein, B., Carey, P. & Jones, K. (1966). Specific semantic word categories in aphasia. *Cortex*, 2: 74-89.

Weingartner, H. (1985). Models of memory dysfunctions. In Olton et al. (1985).

Chapter 13—Amnesia

See: Hirst, W. (1982). The amnesic syndrome: Descriptions and explanations. *Psychological Bulletin*, 91: 435-60.

Warrington, E. K. & Shallice, T. (1972). Neurophysiological evidence of visual storage in short-term memory tasks. *Quarterly Journal of Experimental Psychology*, 24: 30-40.

211—memory consolidation can persist for years, Squire (1986).

212—adrenalin/arousal experiment, Christianson, S-A et al. (1984). Physiological and cognitive determinants of emotional arousal in mediating amnesia. *Umea Psychological Reports*, 176: 19.

213—for Freud on repression see especially Freud, S. (1914a). Remembering, repeating and working-through. In *The standard edition*, ed. & trans., James Strachey, vol. 12. London: Hogarth Press. Freud, S. (1914b). The history of the psychoanalytic movement. In *The standard edition*, ed. & trans., James Strachey, vol. 14. London: Hogarth Press.

214—K. F.'s forgetting of complex instructions, Warrington & Shallice (1972).

215—the basic story of H. M. is set forth in: Milner, B. (1959). The memory deficit in bilateral hippocampal lesions. *Psychiatric Research Reports*. pp. 43-58; Milner, B., Corkin, S. & Teuber, H-L. (1968). Further analysis of the hippocampal amnesic syndrome: fourteen-year follow-up study of H. M. *Neuropsychologica*, Vol. 10, 215-34.; Milner, B. (1970). Memory and the medial temporal regions of the brain. In Pribram, K. H. & Broadbent, D. E. (eds). *The biology of memory*. New York: Academic Press.

216—Ribot's conjecture, Hirst (1982), pp. 453-4.

216—retrograde amnesia is a failure of cues and severity is time dependent, Riccio, D. C. & Richardson, R. (1984). The status of memory following experimentally induced amnesias: Gone but not forgotten. *Physiological Psychology*, 12: 59-72.

217—general memory in amnesics is nearly normal, Schacter, D. L. & Graf, P. (1986). Effects of elborative processing on implicit and explicit memory for new associations. *Journal of Experimental Psychology: Learning, Memory, and Cognition*, 12: 432-44.

217—amnesics quickly generalize from lists, Warrington & Shallice (1972).

217—amnesics forced recognition is good, Hirst (1982) p. 442; Hirst, W., Johnson, M. K., Kim, J. K., Phelps, E. A., Risse, G., & Volpe, B. T.

(1986). Recognition and recall in amnesics. Journal of Experimental Psychology: Learning, Memory, and Cognition, 12: pp. 445-451.

218—H. M. and stylus maze, Milner, B. & Taylor, L. (1972). Right-hemisphere superiority in tactile pattern recognition over cerebral commisurotomy: evidence for nonverbal memory. *Neuropsychologia,* 10: 1-15. See also: Milner, B. (1966) Amnesia following operation on the temporal lobes. In C. W. M. Whitty & O. L. Zangwill, eds. *Amnesia.* London: Butterworth.

218—typical causes of amnesia, Corkin, S, Cohen, N. J., Sullivan, E. V., Clegg, R. A., Rosen, T. J., & Ackerman, R. H. (1985). Analyses of global memory impairments of different etiologies. In Olton et al. (1985). See also: Parkin, A. J. (1984). Amnesic syndrome: A lesion-specific disorder? *Cortex,* 20: 479-508.

219—Korsakoff patient fears hand, Klatzky, R. L. (1984). *Memory and awareness: An information-processing perspective.* New York: W. H. Freeman and Company, p. 1.

219—Korsakoff patient's emotional growth, Sacks (1985), chap. 2.

219—similarity between infant and amnesic memory, Moscovitch, M. (1985). Memory from infancy to old age: Implications for theories of normal and pathological memory. In Olton et al. (1985), p. 78.

See also: Graf, P. & Schacter, D. L. (1985). Implicit and explicit memory for new associations in normal and amnesic subjects. *Journal of Experimental Psychology: Learning, Memory, and Cognition,* 11: 501-18.

Chapter 14—Forgetting to Remember

See: Freeman, L. (1972). *The story of Anna O.* New York: Walker.

224—rate of fugue in South Pacific, Fisher, C. (1945). Amnesic states in war neuroses: The psychogenesis of fugues. *Psychoanalytic Quarterly,* 14: 437-68. p. 437.

224—story of fugues of A.B., C.D., I.J., *ibid.*

225—case of Louise L's fugue, Venn, J. (1984). Family etiology and remission in a case of psychogenic fugue. *Family Process,* 23: 429-35.

226—James on fugues, cited in *ibid.,* p. 435.

227—story of Anna O, Breuer & Freud (1895).

227—Bertha Pappenheim's letter, Freeman (1972), p. 234.

230—Breuer's work with Anna O failed to help her, see Jones, E. (1953). *The life and work of Sigmund Freud.* Vol. 1. New York: Basic Books; and Freeman (1972).

Chapter 15—Forgetting and Old Age

232—Alzheimer's disease readily misdiagnosed, Filinson, R. (1984). Diagnosis of senile dementia Alzheimer's type: The state of the art. *Clinical Gerontologist,* 2: 3-23.

233—elderly learn artificial memory, Robertson-Tchabo, E. A., Hausman, C., & Arenberg, D. (1976). A class mnemonic for older learners: A trip that works! *Educational Gerontology,* 1: 215-26.

234—elderly people's memory for recent events as good as memory for events from long ago, Kahn, R. & Miller, N. (1978). Adaptational factors in memory function in the aged. *Experimental Aging Research,* 4: 273-89.

234—prompt recall is stable among elderly, Schaie, K. W. & Geiwitz. (1982). Learning and memory: Old dogs, new tricks! In Schaie, K. W. & Geiwitz, J., eds. (1982), *Readings in adult development and aging.* Boston: Little, Brown, p. 297.

235—patients who complain of memory problems show more depression than patients who do not complain, Kahn, R., Zarit, S. H., Hilbert, N. M. & Niederehe, G. (1975). Memory complaint and impairment in the aged: The effect of depression and altered brain function. *Archives of General Psychiatry,* 32: 1569-73.

236—recall declines with age, recognition stable, Schonfield, D. (1965). Memory storage and age. *Nature,* 28: 918.

See also:

Perlmutter, M. (1980). An apparent paradox about memory aging. In Poon, L. W., Fozard, J. L., Cermak, L. S., Arenberg, L. W. (Eds) (1980). *New directions in memory and aging: Proceedings of the George A. Talland Memorial Conference.* Hillsdale, NJ: Lawrence Erlbaum Associates.

Yarmey, A. Daniel (1984). Age as a factor in eyewitness memory. In Wells & Loftus, Eds. (1984).

PART FOUR—THE EXPERIENCE OF MEMORY

Chapter 16—Memory and Life

245—the most common standardized memory test is the *Wechsler memory scale.* Cleveland: Psychological Corporation.

247—lions do not recognize gazelles in trees, Schaller, G. B. (1972). *The Serengeti lion: A study of predator-prey relations.* Chicago: University of Chicago Press.

Chapter 17—The Emotional Memory of John Dean

For the text of Dean's testimony and Watergate tapes see:

Gold, G. (Gen ed) (1973). *The Watergate hearings: Break-in and coverup.* New York: Bantam Books.

Gold, G. (Gen ed) (1974). *The White House transcripts*. New York: Bantam Books.

249—testimony-transcript comparison, Gold (1973), p. 277; (1974), pp. 57-69.

252—Baker-Dean exchange, Gold (1973), p. 355.

254—Nixon vows revenge, Gold (1974), p. 58.

254—Nixon on coverup's purpose, *Ibid.*, p. 66.

254—Nixon gives his authority to coverup, *Ibid.*, p. 67.

255—for Neisser's study of Dean, see Neisser, U. (1981). John Dean's memory: a case study. *Cognition* 9: 1-22.

256—Dean on his newspaper memory method, Gold (1973), pp. 331-2.

256—Dean's original statement on late February meeting with Nixon, *Ibid.*, p. 287.

257—Nixon and Dean on ambition of Senate Watergate Committee, Gold (1974), p. 92.

258—Dean/Gurney exchange over Mayflower Hotel, Gold (1973), pp. 357-9. Dean found morning briefing dull. Dean, J. W. III (1976). *Blind ambition: The White House years*. New York: Simon and Schuster, p. 65.

261—Dean put memory of other helicopter rides out of mind, *ibid.*, p. 14.

262—Dean on the tickler, *Ibid.*, p. 65.

263—Dean habitually masked his emotions, *Ibid.*, p. 12.

263—Dean could control headiness and keep hustling, *Ibid., p. 14.*

263—Dean suppressed interest before any interview, *Ibid.*, p. 15.

264—Dean's defense of DeLoach, Gold (1974) p. 108.

264—frightened staff after Watergate, Dean (1976) note especially p. 113.

Chapter 18—The Factual Memory of S

Entire chapter based on Luria, A. R. (1968). *The mind of a mnemonist: A little book about a vast memory*, trans. L. Solotaroff. New York: Basic Books.

267—S's memory based on perception and attention, *Ibid.*, p. 62.

267—S's problem with remembering learning generalities, Bruner's foreword in Luria (1968), p. viii.

268—weigh one's words, *Ibid.*, p. 120.

269—S did not look for meaning behind memory, *Ibid.*, p. 58.

269—S overlooked logic, *ibid.*p. 98.

270—S was surprised to learn his memory was unusual, *Ibid.*, p. 8.

270—S did not notice order in numbers, *ibid.*, p. 59.

270—S was poor at interpretive recognition, *Ibid.*, p. 64.

271—S could picture things in mind and they happened, *Ibid.*, p. 139.

271—synesthesic description, *Ibid.*, p. 23.

271—crumbly yellow voice, *Ibid., p. 24.*

271—nature of synesthesic blurs, *Ibid.*, p. 22.

272—Eisenstein's voice, *Ibid.*, p. 24.

272—music in restaurants, *Ibid.*, pp. 81-2.

275—S was unusually passive, *Ibid.*, pp. 151-2.

275—S reinvented artificial memory system of spaces, *Ibid.*, pp. 41-45.

276—the secret of forgetting is in desire, *Ibid.*, p. 72.

Chapter 19—The Interpretive Memory of Marcel Proust

279—Sultan Mahomet II, Proust (1981), vol. I, p. 386

280—disorientation in bed, *Ibid.*, vol. I, pp. 4-5.

281—the full scene of the madeleine, *Ibid.*, vol. I, pp. 48-51.

282—Elstir on search for point of view, *Ibid.*, vol. I, p. 233-4.

283—dinner party gaffe, *ibid.*, vol. I, pp. 588, 619.

283—cruelty of memory, *Ibid.*, vol. III, p. 569.

284—memory of arms and limbs, *Ibid.*, vol. III, p. 716.

285—revelations on Marcel's time regained, ("what another person sees . . ." etc.) *Ibid.*, vol. III, p. 932.

286—bad memory encourages study of memory, *Ibid.*, vol. II, p. 676.

288—Contre Sainte-Beuve (1909), English text as *By Way of Sainte-Beuve* (1958). Trans. Sylvia Townsend-Warner. New York: Random House.

INDEX